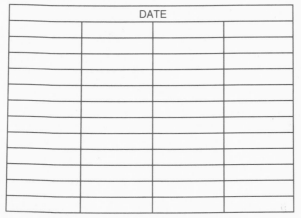

ML
3518
.W66
1994

Woods, Bernie.

When the music
    stopped.

$24.95

DATE			

NOV   1995
BAKER & TAYLOR

WHEN THE MUSIC STOPPED

When the Music Stopped

THE BIG BAND ERA REMEMBERED

by Bernie Woods

BARRICADE BOOKS

NEW YORK

Published by Barricade Books Inc.
150 Fifth Avenue
New York, NY 10011

Printed in the United States of America

Library of Congress Catalog-in-Publication Data
Woods, Bernie.
    When the music stopped: the big band era remembered / by Bernie
Woods.
    p. cm.
    ISBN 1-56980-022-7
    1. Big band music—History and criticism. I. Title.
ML3518.W66 1994
781.65'4—dc20   94-25364
                                                       CIP

First Printing

CONTENTS

CHAPTER I

Introduction

This book is not designed to denigrate those who peopled the great "Era of the Big Bands." Rather it is my intention to faithfully chronicle the lives and loves of the men and women who conducted the overall music industry of that time, as distinct from the completely different world of music in the modern manner.

Things change. That's to be expected. However, when there's change, it is usually for the better. Sadly, I do not believe that has occurred in the music industry. I believe that, excepting for a relative handful of personalities with excellent writing and performing credentials, the level of music industry talent in both those categories has badly deteriorated.

One of the old-time gag lines epitomizes the accepted approach to today's music: "If you can't be good, be loud."

The world I talk about here was wild, sexy, often mad, always interesting, and a lot of fun. It was a solidly professional world that captivated and held close everyone concerned—until rock reared its ugly head and all the fun and frolic went up in the smoke of the weed and the giddiness of coke.

Most of the bandleaders noted here were the standout names of the "Era." I did not make a special effort then to associate only with the stars, but did so because stars make the news and my function was to get and print the news.

I was Music Editor of *Variety*, the theatrical weekly that covers all phases of show business, now nearing its 100th anniversary.

I sought news interesting to the entire music business, which encompassed bandleaders, their booking agencies and executives, songwriters and music publishers, recording executives and their staffs, and the owners and operators of the hundreds of ballrooms, cafes, and hotels from coast to coast, all of whom were involved with and subsisted on the "product" provided by the Big Bands.

CHAPTER 2

Variety

I sat in front of the big radio feeling quite giddy. I'd never had such an exhilarating feeling. I already knew I had two left feet in response to music, but listening to what was coming out of that speaker I thought I might have made up for that with two right ears.

It wasn't the overall Big Band sound that I was appreciating for the first time that got to me; rather it was the way I could plainly hear every nuance of what was being played that had my rapt attention. Each section of the band came through loud and clear. The radio was pouring out one of the most exciting big band compositions ever written—Benny Goodman's theme.

It was 1935 and I had never before heard of big bands or Benny Goodman. I worked at my father's print shop as a messenger. My world was hooking rides, to pocket the carfare, on trucks running east or west on Chambers Street in downtown New York

City, and hooking fresh fruit from open display boxes as I ran through the old Washington Market.

My dad's shop was on old City Hall Place, New York, now the site of Police Headquarters. The main office was at Franklin and Washington Streets a block from the Hudson River piers where the fruit from Central America, for which the shop printed whole-sale auction catalogs, arrived.

I ran like a yo-yo between the two points for a couple of years, meanwhile acquiring other future-polishing skills such as regularly flunking school subjects, spending time in detention rooms, becoming a pool shark good enough to make a living playing nineball (occasionally defeating world-championship contenders in straight-pool exhibition matches), driving sprint and midget race cars under assumed names to escape my father's wrath (his heads of steam were frequent and explosive on almost anything that did not meet his standards), and otherwise showing all the promise of a completely backward youth.

My schooling ended in 1926 at graduation from St. Fidelis Elementary, College Point, Long Island. My dad didn't believe in education, an attitude very likely developed after the birth of my seventh sister (one brother). We needed the twelve bucks a week he was paying me, almost all of which went from one of his pockets to another, which left me to develop my own sources of income—hence the pool-table gambling and racing.

Those aptitudes made it difficult to get out of bed in the early morning, and there came the day when he'd had enough. He fired me. His action thankfully bounced me out of the well of printer's ink that contained him all his life and which might have mired me.

I believe he only intended to scare me into what he termed "responsible behavior," but I didn't wait. The next morning I picked a name out of the *New York Daily Mirror*, the *Wall Street*

Journal of the subway set of that day, and hied myself to an employment agency on Madison Avenue in New York which, I hoped, might come up with a way of making a living that did not involve running errands, hitching onto trucks, or pouring hot lead into molds.

I outlined my "skills" on a job application. A fellow behind a desk scanned my "resume" with the proper perspective. He promptly announced he had an "excellent job"—a post as a messenger which paid two bucks more a week than my dad had been providing and recovering.

When I got to the address—154 West 46th Street just off Times Square—I stood across the street and read the huge one-word sign that occupied the entire plate glass of the old-fashioned ground-level store front. It said, *Variety*.

I'd never heard of it. "What the hell is that?" I asked myself. Nevertheless, I went into what seemed a weird setting. The downstairs floor of the four-story building was walled from front to back with huge mirrors. (The place was once a dress shop and never redone.)

I was interviewed and told to call back at 6 P.M. In my usual front- car-window position on the subway going home, with what I thought was plenty of time to make the call, I spotted a huge clock as we approached the Queens Plaza station. It read 6:05. I raced off the train and down to a phone. Mr. Harold Erichs seemed nonplused when I reached him, but finally agreed I could begin using my fleet feet for *Variety* the following morning at nine sharp.

Months later, I found out why Erichs seemed thrown by my call. He had not intended to give the job to me because I lived "far out" in Queens (12 miles). He had another youngster in mind who lived a few blocks from the office (an area from which he originated). His attitude was based on the fact that errand boys were required to work late certain nights delivering edited copy from the editorial rooms to the press, on Pearl Street just east of Park Row, less than two blocks from my dad's shop. And he felt I might have trouble getting home at late hours.

However, the clock which read 6:05 wasn't telling the truth. This was a few days after clocks had been set back to EST from DST (October 1930) and the huge timepiece I noticed had not yet been revised. Erichs, impressed with the eagerness and enthusiasm I showed by calling him at five instead of six o'clock, gave the job to me. Thus, I was saved from a life of printer's ink.

Little did I realize that in a few years I would be projected into the middle of a scene that began to focus dimly the night I flipped over Benny Goodman's radio broadcast—that there would come a time when I would be looked upon as a respected and knowledgeable member of the exciting music business community, which encompassed then only the great bands, the recording industry, then a smidgen of what it is now, and the music publishing business.

As a *Variety* messenger I found a life always different, always interesting, even from my worm's-eye view. My assignments often involved delivering to or picking up things from the celebrities of that day, all of whom were friends of the founder and owner of *Variety*—Sime Silverman.

I "met" Eddie Cantor, Al Jolson, Ruth Etting, Olsen & Johnson (later of *Hellzapoppin* fame), Burns & Allen, and many more of the older stars in their waning show-biz years. Most were from the heyday of vaudeville, then doing a fast fade. It was an era of show business that spawned the stars of the succeeding level of public acclaim—radio broadcasting. Jack Benny, Bob Hope, Edgar Bergen—virtually every star of the early days of radio sprang from vaudeville.

Speaking of Sime Silverman, the founder of *Variety*, is to speak of rare people. He ran the newspaper with an iron hand and wielded tremendous influence throughout every phase of the show business of his time. He had the power to see men of his choosing installed into high executive positions in various organizations, which gave the paper access to important industry news as well as potential advertising revenues.

Before *Variety* ever reached that level, however, there were years of struggle and privation, punctuated by bitter fights for survival with industry heavyweights who disagreed with *Variety*'s approach to news and, particularly, honest reviews. His disputes with some of the most powerful nabobs in the world of vaudeville and legit (Broadway plays), almost sank the paper.

For no known reason, Sime seemed partial to me as a general "gofer." Very often on Friday and Monday evenings, when the staff was pounding out copy against the paper's Tuesday evening deadline, I would be called to the editorial room. Sime occupied a desk at the rear of the long room, overlooking the clacking typewriters, waiting for copy to edit. As each writer finished a page I would almost literally yank it out of the machine and relay it to Sime.

Sime was tough on his staff men and tough on his errand boys. More than one runner was instantly fired because he could not understand the "ol' boy's" mumbled orders. Sime never lifted his head when he issued instructions, so intent was he on the copy he usually was editing, which made it difficult to understand him. This led to a game among the boys of how to sidestep Sime's summons.

When his number came up on the downstairs callbox (six or so editorial executives also had buzzers to summon boys) they would scatter like a covey of quail facing a barrelful of buckshot. They'd dive down the basement stairs, into the men's room, even out into the street if they were near the door while I did a which-way-did-they-go double-take.

But, the more I got nailed by the buzzer the more I got to know Sime and his needs. He called for very few things—cigarettes, fried egg sandwiches on white (no frills), or to have copy taken to the downtown press. I survived the first few months by concluding that he wanted certain things at certain times of the day. I walked that tightrope for at least four years and never wavered.

Once I answered his buzzer around 4 P.M. and was given a prescription to be taken to a local drug store, where I was informed that the refill potential had expired and a new prescription was required. Back at the office I was intercepted by Harold Erichs, Business Manager and the man who hired me. I explained. His advice: "Tell the boss quick and get the hell out of there."

I felt my inability to bring back what was wanted wasn't my fault so I took my time explaining. Sime's comment was a simple "Oh". Then he slipped me a buck "for coffee." He never bothered to get a new prescription.

As for Sime's toughness, a fair part of it was myth. Perhaps the snap firings were his way of eliminating what he thought were the goofballs among the kids sent over by the agency that serviced us. He frequently showed compassion for his messenger corps. For example: boys worked weekends on *Variety*, mainly to answer telephones, dispense mail (vaudeville performers could use the office as a "mail drop," much like a Post Office box) and run occasional errands, for Sime only. At 4 or 5 P.M. Sunday afternoon he'd have a press trip ready. Very often during the hot summer months he'd ring, hand me envelopes of edited copy and a buck for coffee and add, "Wait for Joe." In a few minutes Sime's huge Locomobile convertible would roll up to the door and chauffeur Joe would be given instructions to drive me downtown to the press and "all the way home." Sime would then take a cab to his Central Park West apartment. He knew the BMT subway ride on a hot August afternoon was a scorcher.

Sime once remarked to editor/reporter Wolfe Kauffman that he had his eye on me as a possible addition to the reportorial staff. Such a thought had never entered my mind. I'd had very little education, could only reflect on the fact that I always got the highest marks in school composition, and was a voracious reader.

Unfortunately, Sime died in 1933 while on a visit to Hollywood, where a daily version of the weekly *Variety* was growing fast. The cause was an extension of the malady for which the druggist had refused a prescription refill.

When I joined *Variety*, in October 1930, a year after the stock market crash that spawned the now classic headline "Wall Street Lays An Egg," Abel Green was manager of the Hollywood office. In December he moved east and became Managing Editor of the weekly. A while later I stepped up from the messenger pool to a position as "copy boy," assistant to Abel, which entailed keeping track of galley proofs of reviews and stories for the next issue, handling revised proofs, and teletyping dispatches culled from the New York staff's daily news roundup to Hollywood's *Daily Variety*.

Abel is the man to whom I owe all possible "kudos," to use one of his favorite words. He was widely known in show business circles and was perhaps the most facile writer I have ever heard. I say "heard" because his typewriter sounded like a machine gun when he was pounding out a story or review.

Abel suggested one afternoon that, if I wasn't doing anything that night, I should stay in town and prowl Times Square. The American Legion was in New York on convention. He felt I might come across interesting items in the nutty behavior of the fun-loving Legionnaires. It was my first, if left-handed, reporter's assignment. I noted the hilarious screwball antics of the veterans, and wrote an item that showed up on the front page, with a by-line.

I was gone. Like the amateur actor digging his first applause, I read my "stuff" over and over. I pasted it on my bedroom wall, in my car, everywhere possible. It's a wonder I didn't do a Milton Berle and paste it on my forehead.

I was ready. Abel wasn't. Not until a year or so later.

On a Wednesday afternoon, most every staff members' day off, I was in the office. Abel called and asked if there was another boy in the office who could handle my job immediately. I went cold. My mind raced. Why did he want a replacement?

I was completely unprepared for his next bomb. "As of tomorrow morning," he stated, "you're a reporter."

My ego shot sky-high, passing on its way up my plummeting confidence, as I suddenly realized the enormity of what had been said to me.

The next morning I was as nervous as the proverbial long-tailed cat in a roomful of rockers, going over my "old job" with the new boy. Abel arrived and bounced up the steps to his front-dais desk. He said "good morning" and nothing else. I waited. Nothing happened. Finally, I stepped up and stood next to him.

"What's up, Bern?" he asked, as though this were an ordinary day.

"I'm ready," I said.

"For what?" he said.

"To be a reporter," I said.

"Oh yeah," he shot back. "Great—go—be a reporter," and he waved at Broadway through the huge window.

Zap! Complete deflation. No bells. No salvo. Not even a boot in the butt.

I went down the stairs and out into the street, first being careful to acquire a pencil and tear some copy paper in half and fold it again, as I'd seen others do, to make notes.

At the corner of 46th and Broadway I stopped and stood. "So I'm a *Variety* mugg," I thought, "What the hell do I do next?"

To understand Abel's wave-off one must understand *Variety*'s routine. There were no story assignments. A reporter dug them out him or herself (there have been female staff members). The only assignments were to review shows.

Rarely did Abel pass on tips to follow. A newsman was hired as a rule to cover a specific section: Motion Pictures, Radio (later Television was added), Music, Vaudeville, or Legitimate (Theater). At the outset I fitted no category. I was a *Variety* bastard, not a mugg. What Abel had done was throw me overboard, possibly to see whether I would drown or come up swimming. I swam.

I drifted in and out of Radio, Vaudeville, and an occasional Music section story. Music was covered by John Hurley, a former errand boy, who preceded me to the editorial floor. When he became seriously ill and spent months in the hospital. Abel assigned me to replace him.

The Big Band era was just starting. I didn't know a soul. One day I met a five-foot whirlwind named Juggy Gayles and soon after a man named Arthur Michaud, a manager of Big Band personalities. Juggy introduced me to songwriters and publishers and Arthur introduced me to bandleaders and booking agency people and I was off and running—make that trotting—it was a while before I was running.

Michaud suggested that I see Tommy Dorsey, then playing the Terrace Room of the New Yorker Hotel. I picked a Saturday night to see Tommy, after attending a Broadway show with my College Point fiancee, Lorraine Swec. The room was jammed. I had just gotten my own *Variety* business cards and sent one to Tommy. I knew he didn't like *Variety* or its people because of something Hurley had written. Tommy was at our table before the set was finished.

From the outset Tommy and I hit it off. Within an hour he'd invited us to his Bernardsville, New Jersey, estate for the weekend. Lorraine was only eighteen at the time and her mother wasn't about to let her spend the weekend with me and a "bunch of wild musicians." Bernardsville had to wait. But, I had established a beachhead with Tommy.

I was twenty-five, weighed less than 120 pounds, looked like an elementary school student, and was scared stiff half the time. I was treading in an area I knew nothing about. I suspect now that the people who befriended me did so because I looked so young and so lost. Tommy's interest, I'm sure, was based on my Irish pan.

I gradually widened my circle of music business contacts. They came from all phases of the industry. Through Juggy I met songwriters Jimmy Van Heusen, then a $60 a week piano player for Remick Music (from which Juggy was then drawing $15 in salary and $10 weekly in expenses.) He had just graduated from "counterboy" to "songplugger." Then Sammy Cahn and Saul Chaplin (just before "Bei Mir Bist Du Schoen"), Lou Levy, manager of the Andrews Sisters, just starting into music publishing, and a host of others.

I was sent by Michaud to see booking agency executives at the powerful Music Corporation of America (MCA). Among these were Willard Alexander, who championed Benny Goodman's style of music and who was a maverick among MCA's top-level group. I met Sonny Werblin, later head of Madison Square Garden (New York), then head of the Monmouth County, New Jersey, race track and still later head of the huge Meadowlands, New Jersey, sports complex. Both were powerful men and full of the kinds of news that *Variety* sought to print.

I made very strong friendships among the major music publishers, some of whom were members of the board of the American Society of Composers, Authors and Publishers (ASCAP), a major source of news to the general music industry of that time. That I played golf fairly well (nine handicap) and knew how to conduct myself at private clubs drew frequent invitations to play from executives who made the news.

As a *Variety* staff man, I was expected to review shows as well as gather news. And my development in this area of "Muggdom" was accelerated by Abel. He force-fed me in the nuances of judging talent and entertainment of all types, starting by assigning me week after week for more than a year to cover burlesque, which at that time was very much alive although, like vaudeville, a fading form. In the Times Square area there were the Eltinge and Republic on 42d Street, the Gaiety at 47th & Broadway, another at 48th & B'way, the Irving Place, downtown, the Star in Brooklyn, and the Hudson in Jersey City. I reviewed two and sometimes three a week and covered each house time and time again.

It took me a while, but I finally managed to understand the purpose. Abel knew that burley comics were still doing many of the great routines from which virtually all comedy emanated. And by cramming me he was providing a groundwork in show business that might otherwise have taken a great deal longer to acquire. The effect lasts until this day, more than fifty years later. It is difficult for me to see any comic situation in films or on TV without conjuring up the original performer and source.

After about a year, I was moved up to vaudeville reviewing and got the same treatment, although there were not too many houses still playing. However, at one time or another I reviewed all the greats, whom I had delivered things to as a messenger: Al Jolson, Eddie Cantor, Ruth Etting, Fred Allen, Jack Benny, Edgar Bergen. I saw the work of Bojangles Robinson, Bob Hope, Weber & Fields, Smith & Dale, Benny Fields, and Blossom Seeley.

I was assigned often to the Apollo Theater on 125th Street in Harlem where I caught all the black greats in comedy, as well as singers and dancers and big bands. Pigmeat Markham, Moms Mabley, Buck & Bubbles, the Nicholas Bros., Miller Bros. & Lois, The Four Chocolates, Duke Ellington, Chick Webb, and Jimmy Lunceford's great bands, Earl Hines, Fats Waller and others, many of whom also played the so-called white theaters.

It really means nothing, but I was the first to review Jerry Lewis and Dean Martin on their first booking after joining forces. Working as singles in 1949 at the 500 Club, Atlantic City, neither was doing much in show business until they began heckling each other. That became so hilarious they combined. When they appeared on the stage of Loew's State on Times Square in conjunction with the film *The Jolson Story* I flipped over their antics, not knowing at the time of their 500 Club success.

Then I moved to night clubs. Edith Piaf, Maurice Chevalier, Hildegarde (rarely did anyone but Abel review her). I reviewed Danny Kaye on what I believe was his first New York club booking in a downstairs nightclub on 57th Street near Fifth Avenue called "La Martinique," from which booking he got a part in a smash Broadway musical. He had spent a great deal of time "preparing" in the New York Catskill Mountains.

There came a time, however, when if I saw my name posted to catch an old-timer, I got disgusted. Until I was assigned to review yiddish theatre actress Molly Picon. All that Abel had forced into me in the past few years suddenly added up. Molly Picon drew my complete admiration for her talent and show business savvy. She and the Jolsons, Cantors, Benny Fields, and the legions of others were complete pros. They often were corny, they often milked, but they played an audience like a great musician plays an instrument. To paraphrase an old song "Every Little Movement Has a Meaning All Its Own."

An angle of reviewing shows that Abel and other staffers had developed, I accomplished in a very negative way. They wrote reviews with only a program to jog their reactions and comments. I always took notes—until I ran into the Irving Place Burlesque, a particularly obscene house. Week after week they put on shows based on low bathroom humor. I gave the writing a once-over every time I was assigned there. Until the night I stepped up to the box office for my press pass and was told to, "Get lost, we don't want you in the theater." I promptly purchased a ticket.

During the show, an arm came over my shoulder and snatched the notes from my hand while a voice over the other shoulder asked whether I'd prefer walking or being carried out.

I walked. "The mob" owned the house.

From that point on I developed a very accurate memory and wrote reviews from a word or two on a program.

All this time the Big Band business was in low gear, but poised to explode. Vaudeville was virtually dead and burlesque was relegated to the sleaze category. So, within a very short time, the big film houses in every major city were featuring big band shows, usually working from a theater's pit elevator. Stage space thus was at a premium, consequently the only vaudeville people who could find bookings were those who worked in "one," mostly comedians.

"Flash" acts and those that required "two", "three" and "four" staging (deeper and deeper) went down the drain or into circuses. (Edgar Bergen's ventriloquist act required full stage. He went into radio.) Dancers had a chance if they could tailor their routines to confined areas.

When the big bands took over the nation's entertainment spotlight they became "the only game in town." There was little other live talent available. Broadway shows were more or less confined to Broadway. Traveling a legit production easily from city to city, as happens now, simply wasn't possible. And with vaudeville gone, small cities and towns were left without live talent until the big bands racked up a fan following and began playing small-town ballrooms and colleges as well as the major-city theaters and hotels.

It was about this time that John Hurley became seriously ill and Abel designated me as "The Music Man." I didn't know my ass from third base. I had no musical training of any kind. I was one of nine kids. Music lessons never entered anyone's mind. They liked to eat.

I took to it like a bee to honey. I was ecstatic all the time. There was excitement, something new every minute, day and night. The feeling generated within me by that first Benny Goodman broadcast was now constant. I couldn't wait to get into the office every morning. How lucky could one get? No schooling beyond the eighth grade, no special training in writing, no musical education and here I was a reporter for a newspaper known the world over, covering an area of show business that was beginning to grab the country and many parts of the world by the ears.

At a rare suggestion from Abel I went one morning to see George Marlo, General Professional Manager of DeSylva, Brown & Henderson, one of the most powerful music catalogs.

And George introduced me to sex in the music industry.

Every once in a while during our conversation he'd twitch or roll his eyes. Funny, I thought, Abel never mentioned an affliction. Suddenly, George seemed to collapse back into his chair, close his eyes, and rest a moment. Then I dug why. He had a broad in the well of his desk giving him "head" as we talked. To the possibly uninitiated, the phrase means she was providing a bit of oral sex. I fell down when he helped her up. He took us both to lunch.

Marlo was one of the best-loved executives in the publishing business and one of its most able. He was a gagster *par excellence*. He delighted in setting up elaborate put-ons and ribs. One of his better gags has been done over and over, with variations. It's called "The Countess" and is one of the undying stories of the music business.

This was in the mid-30's. Paul Whiteman, the most widely known bandleader of his day and a handy man with a female, was opening at the Roosevelt Grill, one of the premier events of the season. Marlo's date was a stunning brunette, tall, willowy, fashionably dressed, wearing a tiara. She had an accent. She threw the group surrounding Whiteman into a tizzy, so attractively did she dominate the party.

At dinner, the "Countess" was seated next to Whiteman. His wife Margaret was on his other side. The wine and the conversation flowed. Whiteman was being gallant to the beauties on both sides. He paid particular attention to the Countess. She was something new.

Suddenly, Whiteman jumped. He'd been groped. Margaret looked at him. It had happened so fast that Whiteman wasn't sure. A few minutes later, another fast grope. A third time and this time the groper held on to his jock. It was the Countess. Whiteman damned near choked on his teeth; wife Margaret was right next to him. Too, he still believed, George told me, that the gal was straight and a real Countess.

The Countess actually was one of the city's highest-priced hookers. Marlo had hired, clothed her, and provided the tiara—all for a gag. He told me the whole deal cost him $500, big money in those times. After the meal, George took Margaret to Lindy's, while Whiteman, "too tired" after undergoing the amenities of an opening night, took the Countess to bed. There could have been no other ending to the evening.

Marlo was the engineer of a Tommy Dorsey bit involving two gals with pubic hair shaved to form his initials. He and Tommy were very close. They both were great pinochle players. Since George was not married, he spent almost every weekend at Tommy's Bernardsville home, if Tommy was there. A gentleman, gracious host, raconteur, roue, virtually every adjective that could be applied to a virile, unmarried male who didn't have a mean bone in his body, could be applied to George Marlo. He knew his business thoroughly and was outstandingly successful.

Most of the music men, be they publisher/owner, general professional manager, or songplugger were hardworking and conscientious. There were a great many characters, however, who kept things hopping in leisure hours. Usually, sex was involved.

Walter Fleischer was an excellent voice coach and accompanist. But, any girl he worked with ran the risk of being talked into bed or onto her knees for a bit of oral sex, the ultimate result of which, she was convinced by Walter's blandishments, would oil and help her vocal cords and make her a much better singer. Or, she'd wind up on her butt while Walter did the munching. He'd eat a doorknob.

The best story told about Fleischer is a gag he arranged to greet some friends due in his office on an appointment. He instructed his secretary to buzz him twice when his guests arrived, wait a few minutes, then send them right on in. When they entered Walter was standing, tickling an upright piano's keys, while a gal sat on the lid. He was eating her like a watermelon and her toes were playing obbligatos on the keys as she popped a few orgasms.

Fleischer was far from being alone. Occasionally, the group I often went to dinner with would run into some of the "head" men and they'd extend an invitation to watch "dessert" being eaten in someone's office. It meant that Walter, Goldie Goldmark, Lester Simms, and one or two other followers of the "Grail Clitoris" were staging an exhibition/contest. They'd rounded up some willing gals (secretaries, singers, etc.), who'd spread-eagle and, at a signal, tongues would flash and the lashing began. The gal who screamed and creamed first would give the win to her man.

The man generally granted to be the premier clitoris polisher in all of musicdom was a major recording company executive named Mitch Miller. Publishers currying his favor would bring hookers or interested amateurs to his Columbia Records office at any hour of the day. He'd make a nympho beg for mercy. Once a publisher friend of mine served him at 11 a.m. with a $100 hooker. She begged the publisher to get the exec away from her after her tenth orgasm.

When talent was brought to him, he'd simply lock his office, which was lined with black drapes all around the room. The steno "bull-pen" was just outside. All the secretaries knew what was "going down." The mental picture of the happenings behind that door caused many a "matinee" among the secretaries and male employees, some of whom lived just a few blocks away on Eighth and Ninth Avenues and could run home for "lunch."

Another great character was a songplugger/voice coach named Mickey Addy. He had been a piano player in a New Orleans bordello and was a strong man with the females. The story about Mickey's peccadillos I like best concerns the night he and a girl friend stopped at his office to pick something up before heading home to the sack. They couldn't wait. Mickey was banging her on his glass-topped desk when the glass shattered and slashed her wiggling bottom. At 2 a.m. Mickey had to dash out, holding an unfulfilled jock, to find an all-night drug store for materials to staunch the blood and make her presentable enough to get to a hospital to have her furrowed fanny stitched.

Addy was a glib Master of Ceremonies. And he loved being a ham. He'd put on his act faster than Berle. And he did a fantastic Baron Munchausen sound-alike. His abilities led him to vacation-time master-of-ceremonies jobs on cruise ships. On one he used the Munchausen take-off exclusively. He got involved with a German-speaking matron from Detroit and even in the sack he'd be urging her on with Baronisms. When they said goodbye, Mickey gave her a send-off in impeccable English. She fainted.

There were countless others in the music biz who followed fine-tuned sex routes, but discreetly because they had wives to go home to. One pair, one of whom is now an important rock/music publisher while the other has passed on, would work together on the nympho secretary of another recording company executive. They tried more ways of working out gang sex than Masters and Johnson could devise with a jig saw.

Another of my favorite stories directly concerns me and my wife only because it epitomizes the average music man's attitude toward anything in skirts, particularly new faces, all of whom were "possibles."

I had reviewed a show and then cabbed it to the Gotham Hotel to see Manie Sachs, head of Columbia Records, to check a story. He needed one body to fill out an eight-against-eight gin game.

I'd forgotten it was Thursday, when Manie ran weekly gin sessions, so I got sucked in nicely. In ten minutes I picked up $80 and ran, having gotten my story. But I was late meeting Lorraine, who'd been shopping. When I arrived at the Cafe Rouge of the Statler Hotel she was at a table of publisher friends. Right behind me as I entered was George Pincus. Lorraine was dancing and as she went by she blew a kiss. She looked gorgeous—tall, slender, and fashionably dressed. George didn't know her.

Seeing a new face and without thinking, Pincus leaned over and whispered, "Who's the cunt?"

Without batting an eye I asked,"You don't know her?"

George came right back, "No, but I'd love to."

"When the set's over I'll introduce you," I said.

When it ended, Lorraine returned and we kissed. Then I said, "Honey, I'd like you to meet George Pincus." George brightly stepped up and ran full tilt into my next line—"George, this is my wife."

George went out the door so fast he spun John, the maitre d', like a top. For years afterward every time Pincus went to Chicago, his home town, he`d send Lorraine a box of a certain brand of chocolate turtles, available only there.

George was General Professional Manager of Shapiro-Bernstein, a powerful music catalog of the time. He subsequently set up his own business and in the process signed an alliance with an English publisher. A few years later the publisher became the British outlet for the initial Beatles hits. The U.S. rights accrued to George, who gathered up money faster than he and his nice wife could count it.

While a great deal of sex went on in the music biz of the 30's and 40's, it was different from other industries only in that it seemed easier to come by. The big band era was a glamorous time

that lured models and secretaries, even from the garment industry, where sex was a work-a-day staple.

Bandleaders and male singers caused women of all ages, married and unmarried, to quickly develop round heels, often to their
amazement. Women who only fantasized sex outside home would
literally leap into the sack with top names. And if the glamour
boys weren't available, some gals would go down the pecking
order of a big-name's entourage. Gals who never thought of trying
oral sex would lip an erection like a popsicle.

Some music men were egotistical and brash. They were accustomed to "pushovers," consequently carried that attitude into other
areas of life. Sometimes it worked; sometimes they got into trouble.

On my way from New York to California I had made arrangements with Joe Shribman, manager of Rosemary Clooney and
Tony Pastor's Orchestra, to join me out of Chicago and share a
bedroom on the Santa Fe's Chief. When he showed, with him was
Al Porgie, a New York publisher I knew well as a bit of a wild
man. We were only a few miles out of Chicago and walking
through cars to the lounge when we passed a stateroom occupied
by a prim, attractive, well-dressed, thirty-ish looking woman who
sat reading a book. Porgie was behind me and I heard him stop.
Curious, I stopped too, just in time to see him lean into the room,
point a finger and say, "I'm going to fuck you tonight." I took off
like a scared rabbit, catching and pushing Joe ahead of me in the
narrow aisle. I wanted no part of the aftermath of that statement.

The result: He did. Porgie spent the next two days in her digs,
the two coming out only occasionally to eat.

When we reached Pasadena, I left the train, inviting both Joe
and Al to ride into Hollywood in a Paramount Pictures limo Abel
had arranged to meet me. While waiting for our baggage I heard
my name called, turned to see a *Daily Variety* staff man running

toward us from two cars away. "Hey, Bern," he yelled, "I didn't know you were coming out. Why didn't you drop me a line?"

It suddenly occurred to me to ask why he was there. He explained, "I came to pick up my wife. She's been in Chicago visiting her sick mother." He introduced us to Porgie's playmate of the past two days.

The music business was not all fun and frolic, however. It was run with iron hands by the "Old Guard," the publishers who had organized ASCAP, the organization which stemmed the rampant use of music for profit without paying royalties. Even today there are entrepreneurs who cannot believe they must pay for the use of copyrighted music. ASCAP'S files are full of the outcome of legal actions (the penalty for illegal use is $250 per song per performance) in which the violators were indignant at having to pay for something they believed should be as free as the air.

In the days of which we write, songs were written by songwriters, published by publishers, and promoted by professional staffs. The income from a hit song was considerable (a pittance compared with modern returns) shared among the publisher and the writers, both of whom drew additional money from ASCAP's licensing efforts. A publisher's staff was well paid and most drew weekly expense checks for which they did not have to account. Some spent the money as it was intended, entertaining anyone— singer, bandleader, radio producer—who could possibly help make a song a hit. Others banked a good part of it and still others spent it on having fun.

It was a wacky, sexy musical world that captivated and held all who peopled it. But, in contrast to the way the modern music industry operates, there was very little dependency on anything except booze. And the use of that stimulant was most often confined to nighttime antics.

In short, the overall music industry of the 30's and 40's capti-vated and held all who peopled it—until rock reared its ugly head and all the fun went the way of the loud, overpowering beat and the often unintelligible one-word lyrics.

Thank the lord for Country Music.

CHAPTER 3

Benny Goodman

Benny Goodman's great band was already the most popular orchestra in America when I inherited the music mantle at *Variety*.

Benny was one of the few leaders with whom I had limited contact. Like Jimmy Dorsey, Benny Goodman seemed to me to be a "musician's musician" in that he appeared to be uncomfortable away from the bandstand. For me, he was hard to talk with, which was strange since I didn't have that problem with other leaders. That didn't bother me. All I wanted was to listen to his great band. To this day, I have never heard anything to equal it for sheer excitement. Duke came within a whisker. Artie Shaw, Tommy Dorsey, Woody Herman's Third Herd, Stan Kenton, and Count (Bill) Basie were all great bands, but none approached the sheer ecstasy of big band sound generated by the Benny Goodman Orchestra.

Benny had class. To my knowledge he never concerned himself with reviews or stories that were not favorable. The one time he ever said anything to me about something I wrote stemmed from one of the most interesting weeks in the history of the band business.

Artie Shaw had just hit hard with his exciting arrangement of "Begin the Beguine." Since Artie also played exciting clarinet, equal in many ways to Benny, there was a similarity in the two bands. General Artists Corporation (GAC), Artie's booking agency, set out to "dethrone" Benny and install Artie in the mythical number one spot.

MCA booked Benny into the Adams Theater in Newark for a one-week stand. Hearing about it, GAC spotted Artie at the rival Paramount Theater, a few blocks distant, to set up a confrontation. The box office clash of the titans stirred tremendous interest. To make it more intriguing, the two bands were surrounded by no-name acts (almost identical in type) and nondescript support films. The bookings were day and date (opened and closed the same days).

I was assigned to review both shows and write a composite story, plus reviews of the two shows. I had difficulty finding a seat in either theater, the fan response to each was so overwhelming. (The two theater managers must have been in cahoots for the benefit of the box office. It was possible to catch Shaw's show, then run and catch Goodman's. I'm certain that added to the b.o. take.) *Variety* went to press on Tuesday afternoon. Just before the final lockup we checked the totals of money drawn to the box office of each theater. Shaw did slightly better than Benny but, I pointed out, Benny Goodman's Adams Theater was on a narrow side street while Shaw's Paramount was on the main drag and had a larger seating capacity. "Drop-ins" could more than cause the slight discrepancy. That info was carried in a small box on the front page.

Goodman surprised me by calling a few days later to say he thought I'd done an excellent job of reporting the entire incident, and particularly thanked me for citing the differences in theater location and seating, which actually were major points in show business reporting.

I was privileged to review Benny's legendary Carnegie Hall concert in January 1938, an event that made such an impact on the music scene that it is still mentioned frequently in reminiscences of the big band era. I was still new to my *Variety* role and somewhat inexperienced. But I flipped. All that was required to understand that Benny Goodman was putting on a performance that would likely live forever was a pair of ears. The evening was fantastic, the audience response ecstatic. Columbia recordings of that concert are among the greatest big band records ever made. They are as exciting now as the first day they were released.

Benny was both respected and envied by his rivals. Most knew him intimately since they all emanated from the same source—New York radio broadcast studios of the early 30's. I once asked Tommy Dorsey what he thought. "I wish I had his band," he answered. At the time, Tommy Dorsey had his great "Song of India" combination.

Benny Goodman had another great distinction. He was the first white leader to feature black musicians. They helped immeasurably to make the band so exciting. Pianist Teddy Hill, guitarist Charley Christian (who died while with the band), and vibraphonist-drummer-pianist Lionel Hampton were tremendous performers. Each was an outstanding soloist as well as integrating with the whole.

Benny stumbled only once in his entire career. In the late 1940's he formed a bop band, which he debuted in Syracuse, New York at the Syracuse Hotel. Hal Davis, his promotion man (later one of the city's outstanding advertising company executives), as strong in his field as Tommy Dorsey's Jack Egan, planned the debut of the band with as much fanfare as possible. He packed some fifty New York based tradepapermen and music publisher friends of Benny into a DC-6 and flew them to Syracuse for the debut. (The trip was a little scary at one point. Landing after dark, the pilots apparently were not familiar with the Syracuse area. They came in real low, dropped gear, then gunned it and did it over again on the other side of town.)

The "bop" band was not bad. Benny was too good a musician to present anything not up to standard. But it was not Benny Goodman.

Goodman was known to virtually all musicians of the Big Band era as "The Ray." The explanation was simple. If any of his musicians goofed interpreting the wonderful Fletcher Henderson arrangements, Benny would bend a withering, baleful eye in his direction. They never forgot. I've heard ex-Benny Goodman men time and again refer to his method of keeping his musicians conscious of what they were doing.

Benny had one association I could never fathom. On *Billboard* at least part of the time I was on *Variety* was a writer named Hal Webman. A B.S. artist of the first water, he got little respect as a writer or a personality.

In 1953, after leaving *Variety* to co-manage the Ralph Flanagan Orchestra, and subsequently shedding that setup, I was looking for office space to conduct my own management business. I ran into Webman. He was intent on organizing a music publishing firm with the financial backing of Benny Goodman, of all people. He had leased a large office and was seeking a co-tenant. It wasn't difficult for him to talk me into it, in spite of how I felt about him.

One day Webman introduced me to his wife. I was flabbergasted. The man was a miracle worker. A perfect five-by-five, he'd married Racquel Gordon, the daughter of top songwriter Mack Gordon, a tall, beautiful, extremely attractive girl who'd been finished at good schools. Months later, I arrived at the office one morning to find Webman in tears. Rac had walked out. The day before, she'd moved everything out of their apartment except his bed. Not too much later, the Benny Goodman connection snapped. Webman was down, way down.

A couple years later I ran into Webman on Broadway. He was hand in hand with a woman a head taller than he whom I recognized immediately. She had been private secretary to Larry Spier when Spier was General Professional Manager of Chappell Music, perhaps the standout publishing house in all musicdom. Webman had just married the gal.

Spier had left Chappell and established his own publishing firm, but he had died and left the firm and his assets to the secretary and his partially handicapped son.

My point is simple. I bow in the man's direction. Shades of Marty Melcher.

But, to get back to Benny Goodman, this was one leader of a great band who was a complete professional. He was hard on his musicians when they goofed, but that discipline made the band what it was—the greatest. I got enormous kicks out of reviewing his performances, both with the band and the classical group he performed with in New York's staid Town Hall.

As one may gather, there is no question in my mind that the Benny Goodman Orchestra, which I first heard on radio about 1935, was the greatest of all the big bands. The only outfit that came close was the Duke Ellington Orchestra—really close.

CHAPTER 4

Tommy Dorsey

Close behind Benny in popularity in the late 30's and early 40's came the great Tommy Dorsey Orchestra.

Tommy was a tremendous individual musician on trombone, as was his brother Jimmy, on sax. The two had once led a band together but, like many brothers, could never see eye-to-eye. They were always battling, had some dillies over the years, but none as widely publicized as the Two-Round-Main at the Astor Hotel in New York.

Tommy started by whacking Jimmy on the chin and depositing him on his butt. But Jimmy bounced up as though he had springs in his rear and the two world-famous leaders mixed it up like a pair of six-year-olds in a hall bedroom. Neither did much damage.

The occasion was an Astor Roof Garden opening of Tommy's band. Because of a run of hit records that included "Green Eyes," "Amapola," "Tangerine," and a few others, Jimmy was almost as popular and working the Strand Theater, just a few blocks north of the Astor.

Jimmy was at Tommy's opening to pay his respects to a brother bandleader who just happened to be his brother. The two had not been very friendly in past months, which really was nothing new. It had been thus since Tommy got up in the middle of a set after an on-stand argument at the Glen Island Casino, New Rochelle, New York, in 1937, left the original Dorsey Brothers Orchestra, and set about building his own band. Within a year or so and for a couple of years thereafter Tommy overshadowed Jimmy, a fact that did not sit well with him, although I never once heard him disparage his brother or the Tommy Dorsey Orchestra.

The table at which Jimmy was sitting was hosted by Rocco Vocco and Jack Bregman, co-owners with Chester Conn of the Bregman-Vocco-Conn music publishing house. Joe Bigelow, writer of the Edgar Bergen-Charlie McCarthy radio show and a former *Variety* staffer, was a guest. I joined them only an hour before closing from the nearby *Variety* offices, where I'd been writing music business stories and reviews, preparing for the paper's Tuesday 4 P.M. press deadline.

The brawl began when Tommy approached the table a few seconds after his closing set. He had avoided the group all evening—a breach of etiquette. To avoid visiting with an important personality, brother or not, was a distinct no-no. And Tommy had done that deliberately. What made his action more obvious was that Rocco was his very close friend. Tommy demanded to know what Jimmy was doing there. Before he could answer Tommy added, "And keep your goddamned manager out of here, too." This was a reference to Billy Burton, sitting across the room in conversation with Jimmy's attorney. Tommy disliked Burton intensely, partly because of a suspicion that Billy, who handled Jimmy's income, was not giving Jimmy a good financial shake. Tommy's attitude was based on the way Billy spent money, which I knew was like water. He felt not all of it could be Burton's own.

Tommy suggested that if Jimmy and Burton did not stay away from the Astor, the next time Jimmy showed up Tommy would delight in punching his nose. Jimmy slowly crushed his cigarette, just as slowly stood up, and made a suggestion of his own. "There's no time like the present, Harve," said Jimmy, using T.D.'s pet name for other people.

Zap, and we were all in the middle. Chairs went flying. Rocco drew a welt on the side of his nose. He was a fast five two and built like a beer barrel. I got bounced on the seat of my pants by a sweep of Tommy's arm.

At last the two were separated. After ties and clothing were adjusted and hair smoothed we headed for the elevators while Tommy disappeared into the dressing rooms behind the bandstand. As we stood waiting, Tommy came out of the back entrance, also headed for the elevator. He was so angry he hadn't stopped for anything except his jacket. Jimmy loudly cracked something I didn't get with his funny giggle. Bam, we were off and running again. But, this one was just a skirmish.

I sat on the "story" overnight. I was tight with Tommy and tight with Burton and, to a certain extent, with Jimmy. Promotion-conscious Billy wanted me to detail the battle. Jimmy asked me not to. Since I already was in the doghouse with Tommy over something else I had written, his feelings at that point were not important.

After sizing up every aspect of the "two-round main" at the Astor, I decided there was entirely too much human-interest in the story to ignore it, no matter who might wind up with a nose out of joint. The media was bound to pick it up sooner or later.

The point of the affair was not two bandleaders in a fight, it was two brothers—each famous bandleaders—in a fight. Brothers have been fighting since Cain and Abel. But this was no pillow putsch in a hall bedroom. This was between two top-level entertainers known the world over; two million-dollar-a-year musicians who, because of their initial dispute, were striving always to top one another with bigger-selling hit recordings, higher ballroom box-office grosses, higher theater salaries. Rivalry all the way down the line.

I was with Jimmy and Burton on a one-nighter at the Sunnybrook Ballroom in Pottstown, Pennsylvania, when Billy determined the band's gross for the evening was only $300 short of Tommy's all-time record for the huge ballroom. He promptly went to the box office and bought $350 worth of admissions, thereby topping Tommy's gross. The Sunnybrook held 6,000 dancers, one of the largest ballrooms anywhere.

The original Dorsey Brothers orchestra had been booked by General Artists Corporation (GAC), then the second-largest band-booking agency in the business. Jimmy stayed with GAC. Tommy signed with MCA. Jimmy was recorded by Decca Records, then perhaps the last label in importance. Tommy signed with RCA-Victor, then the largest.

When *Variety* hit the stands on Wednesday morning, 36 hours after the embroglio, I was on the golf course with Perry Como, George Paxton, then a bandleader-arranger, and Tommy Valando, General Professional Manager of Santly-Joy Music Co. I was called off the course twice by urgent telephone calls, the first by an editor of the *New York Journal-American*, New York's Hearstchain flagship, who dug the human side of the Dorsey story. He wanted additional information and had called *Variety*, who referred him to my home; Lorraine referred him to the Old Bayside, New York, links where we were hacking around.

The second call was from Tommy, who in no uncertain terms informed me as to the sort of s.o.b. I had become.

That evening the Dorsey Brothers swing-fest hit the front pages of every Hearst paper across the country. Jimmy never said a word. Burton acted like the cat that made off with the canary.

Tommy made me feel like it had been worth risking the various friendships when weeks later he called from Hollywood to tell me that my story, as circulated by the Hearst papers, provided him and Jimmy with more publicity than either had ever had before. Tommy had worked across country toward an opening at the Palladium Ballroom in Hollywood, and found fans warmed toward both brothers as never before. Dancers, said T.D., were friendlier and much more responsive.

A psychiatrist, perhaps, would say that the battle made both Tommy and Jimmy appear to be "one of us" rather than untouchable stars to their legions of fans.

In the late 30's and 40's Big Band leaders were American royalty. There was very little live entertainment in the small cities and towns that housed the nation's large ballrooms. And when a prominent band, one they'd heard on radio broadcasts from the big cities, came to town, it was a big event.

Tommy knew also that anything that added to Jimmy's charisma was a huge plus. Tommy always had what Jimmy lacked. He had oodles of stage presence, warmth, personality, and know-how. Jimmy, to me, always seemed uncomfortable before an audience unless he had a horn in his hands. Tommy understood crowded ballrooms; he set tempos that were easy and flowing. Jimmy often kicked off tempos that were awkward, which was part of what caused the breakup of the original Dorsey Brothers Orchestra. The two men were inverted then: Jimmy was up front. Tommy should have led the band.

The source of most of the two brothers' problems was music publisher "friends" seeking advantages with one brother or the other. To curry favor with either, some publishers would report to them anything that one Dorsey might have said in anger about the other, often in response to something the other was purported to have said, as relayed by another tale-bearer.

After the fight, the two brothers stayed enemies until the death of their father, the man who fostered their development as musicians. Over their father's bier they agreed that, if either was told of something derogatory the other supposedly had said, the injured party was to immediately find the other, and check.

The solution worked.

Tommy was one of the more astute businessmen among the top name bandleaders. In his early days he was managed by Arthur Michaud, but when I met him Tommy was handling his own affairs, abetted by accountant Phil Braunstein, who later became my accountant and good friend. While I was on *Variety*, Phil was a solid source of news, since he handled the financial affairs of a number of bands.

Tommy led a really good band. He stocked it with the best musicians available and had outstanding arrangers such as Paul Weston, who later married Jo Stafford, Axel Stordahl, and later the great Sy Oliver. The combination turned out a long string of hits on RCA-Victor records, instrumentals as well as the tremendous vocal hits with Frank Sinatra and the Pied Pipers.

The band jumped, especially when Buddy Rich was on drums.

Tommy was brainier than most other leaders. When he was in front of a band that for some reason wasn't up to what he felt it should be, he hid the whole thing behind his great trombone. There are many examples of this on the early Victor platters, some almost entirely a trombone solo.

Tommy could never be considered a rich man despite his annual income. He frequently advanced money to help others develop. On a 5 A.M. Sunday morning ride from the Statler Hotel in New York to his Bernardsville, New Jersey, estate where we were to spend the weekend, Tommy told me had advanced more than $60,000 to Glenn Miller to tide that band over. He also advanced money to fund the Bob Chester Orchestra despite the fact that Chester's mother was married into the wealthy Fisher Body family of Detroit (General Motors).

Tommy also provided Frank Sinatra with seed money when Frank left the band, in return for a piece of his future earnings. It was bruited about that the piece was returned after heavy mob pressure was brought to bear on T.D. I had no knowledge of the deal. I always felt such agreements between performers were not viable *Variety* news items. I did not ever ask Tommy for details.

One afternoon late in 1944, I was sitting with Tommy in his huge offices on the top floor of the Brill Buildings. He showed me a check for $33,000 from the IRS. It was a refund on his taxes. He had a second check for $25,000 signed by a top star of that time, the return of a loan T.D. had made. Tommy said to me, "With this cash I now have over $300,000." It was more money than he had ever had in his life at one time. For then it was a helluva stash. The hoard didn't last long. A while later it shrank considerably. He gave $250,000 of it to Pat Dane, his second wife, to get rid of her, so he said.

While T.D. was a very astute businessman where his band was concerned, he was a wild man otherwise. He threw money around like confetti. He was a periodic drunk and a nasty one when he was heavily loaded. And he was high as a kite on sex, particularly the oral variety. One of his early vocalists he touted as great "head." She must have been; she obviously was not with the band for her singing ability. He'd frequently be indulged between sets on a dance job.

However, Tommy always described Pat Dane as the "artiste of artistes" at the art of "polishing a knob," a favorite music-man phrase. As a gag, he would often introduce Pat to people as "the world's greatest hat job." A sometime-actress, Pat loved to shock the wives of Tommy's business associates and friends with sex-oriented remarks that left them speechless. Usually the cracks came when they were least expected, making them doubly effective.

At a T.D. opening at Frank Dailey's Meadowbrook in Cedar Grove, New Jersey, one of the band era's outstanding play-dates, Lorraine and I were at a table with Mr. and Mrs. Arthur Michaud, who were so square, and a couple of older publishers and their wives. Tommy sat down between sets. The place was jammed and he was exhausted handling the amenities of an opening. He said he wished the evening was over and he was back at his Bernardsville estate. Pat turned to him while everyone listened and said, "Why? You've had it in as far as it goes—at either end." The lull in the conversation lasted quite a while. Each wife tried hard to regain composure, but it wasn't easy.

I was invited to dinner one evening by T.D. He was working Dailey's Terrace Room in Newark, New Jersey, to which Dailey had moved his Meadowbrook operation because of wartime gasoline restrictions. When I met him at the New York garage we all used, Pat was with him. We reached Dailey's quite early and were the only party in the big room. Later, a group consisting of a father, mother, and daughter about thirteen or fourteen, obviously dyed-in-the-wool big band fans, were seated nearby. When they spotted Tommy, the father sent the girl over for an autograph. The youngster ignored Pat, who liked to feel she was important enough for autographs as a sometime movie personality (mostly bit parts, although she did have one reasonably important role). She was furious at the "slight."

"Autograph, schmautograph, I'll autograph your cock with my teeth when we get home," she said. I thought the youngster could hear the remark and I choked on my soup, spraying half a mouthful over T.D.

One trip I made to Hollywood followed by just a few days the famed "cutting scene" at Tommy's apartment wherein one of his guests at an afternoon soiree knifed another over a remark made to Pat about her sexual prowess. A while later when I visited at the Sunset Plaza apartments above Sunset Boulevard, blood was still on the carpet.

Tommy's band was then working the Palladium Ballroom. But he had had a salary dispute with the ballroom's operators so, being Tommy Dorsey, he went out and bought the Aragon Ballroom, on the boardwalk at Ocean City near Santa Monica, and renamed it Casino Gardens. We drove out one afternoon. He wanted to show me the place and detail his plans for it. It was a huge building (in later years it housed the Lawrence Welk television show). After an hour or so, Tommy suddenly remembered a date he had at home with Ziggy Elman. When we reached the apartment we found Ziggy sitting in one love seat and right opposite in another was Pat, sleep still in her eyes. She had just gotten up to let Ziggy in.

Noting their relative positions, Tommy cracked to Pat, "Did you take care of him while he waited?"

Another time while they were on the coast, Tommy, who often teased Pat unmercifully, told her he no longer thought she was "the greatest." How he knew he didn't say, but he claimed a girl at the Sherman Hotel in Chicago, now defunct but a famed big band spot during "The Era," was a superior performer. Pat blew high and wide, got very upset. Finally, Tommy called the girl who appropriately enough, was a hat checker. He wired her money to come to California to prove his point. She did Tommy, while Pat observed. Not only that, the gal was double-gaited and gave Pat a sample of her clitoris-polishing ability.

Pat had a great body. She loved to flaunt it. She had very white skin. She never ever went out in the sun. She took milk baths, the presumed reason her skin was so white. I know well it was very white because Tommy once invited me to the Statler Hotel, where he was playing, for a Saturday afternoon lunch. "We'll listen to the Notre Dame game (on radio)," he said.

When I got to his suite, Pat was still asleep. When she awoke she made repeated trips across the living room from one bedroom to the other, each time allowing her negligee to stream out behind her.

By the time I finished lunch I was bug-eyed and dry-mouthed.

Tommy and his entourage were great gagsters. He pulled a variation of the Paul Whiteman/George Marlo bit on Sammy Kaye's manager, Jim Peppe, a real gentleman and about as straight-laced as one could find. I knew him for years and cannot recall one foul word from his mouth. He and Sammy were on the coast on business and were invited to the Sunset Plaza apartment for a Sunday morning breakfast.

One of the guests was a very circumspect young lady, braided hair coiled on head. She was introduced as the sister of one of Tommy's men, a schoolteacher from Kansas. She sat prim and quiet. Being the nice guy that he was, Jim engaged her in conversation seeking to make her more comfortable than she looked in this famous company.

She said she didn't like teaching school and wanted to give it up. Naturally Jim asked what she wanted to do. She leaned over, grabbed his zipper and pulled it down. She really wanted to be a prostitute and suck cock, she said, beginning with his.

Tommy told me he thought Jim was having an apoplectic fit as a result and that he really regretted the gag.

Another time Tommy was living at Hollywood Garden of Allah, then a nice place to live for "straight" beings. Kay Kyser had an apartment nearby. Tommy invited him to breakfast, and during the meal maneuvered an argument with Kyser, who also was as straight-laced as a bishop. The meat of the discussion was whose fans were more loyal (Kyser then had "the Kollege of Musical Knowledge" going big for him on network radio).

When the argument waxed real hot, T.D. said "I'll show you some real loyal fans." With that two tall gals came out of a bedroom in robes. They stood side by side naked as jaybirds while Kyser boggled.

The pubic hair on one was cut to spell a "T" while the other was cut to form a "D".

Tommy had a minion named Larry Daniels, who had a reputation as a real nut. Tommy gave a birthday party for one of his people in a room with a small stage. The shindig began when the lights went out, the stage curtains parted and there was Daniels standing on his head, legs outspread, with a lighted candle stuck up his ass.

While a great musician, Tommy was a real artiste in that he was flaky and flighty in many ways. He'd stay away from booze if he had a certain type of soft drink. He carried cases of it along on road trips. Once he ran out in Columbus, Ohio, and George Marlo, his bosom pinochle buddy, hopped a train with a few cases. Tommy once sent a band boy on an airplane from Syracuse to Lindy's in New York, to pick up a bagful of schnecken (sweet rolls in midwestern parlance). When the fellow got back, Tommy wasn't hungry.

The first time I visited Tommy at his Bernardsville estate I looked the place over and, for laughs since I was a golfer, said, "What, no golf course?" I hardly had it out of my mouth before Toots, T.D.'s first wife, and Jack Egan, Tommy's great promotion man who had been with him for years, practically mugged me. "Be quiet," they warned, "or we'll have one next week."

The Bernardsville place comprised nine acres under heavy foliage. It had two electrically driven gates with voice communication, a swimming pool a hundred yards from the house along a path lighted at night (complete with his and her bathhouses), tennis court, handball court, badminton court, and huge outdoor grill. The house itself had six or seven bedrooms, one equipped with enough bunk beds to house the entire band along with a barracks-style bathroom with johns and sinks to accommodate half the band at one time.

Tommy eventually sold this house for $55,000. He told me later that its carpeting and drapes cost him more than the selling price. Today, the estate would be worth three or four million.

During that first visit to Bernardsville Tommy offered me a job. He had started his own newspaper some months before titled, as one would expect, *The Bandstand*. I didn't know it then, but he had gotten a mad on against *Variety* for something written by my predecessor, John Hurley, and revenge would have been sweet if he could have gotten me to go to work for him.

Egan, an astute and very talented promotion man, was running *The Bandstand*, culling material no doubt, from *Variety* and other music sheets, but he could not handle both jobs. So, Tommy wanted a reporter and editor for the sheet.

I knew there was no way I would ever work for T.D. He was a martinet with people under him. I saw the way he treated Bobby Burns, his road manager, and I would never have put myself in a similar position.

I made many trips to Bernardsville, however, because I enjoyed Tommy's company. He had a great Lionel train set, bought for Tommy, Jr., but T.D. typically got the most pleasure out of it.

One weekend in the late 30's T.D. put on a benefit for the Bernardsville Fire Department. Out of his own pocket he bought enough half-inch tongue-and-groove planking to form a crude dance floor almost an acre in size, then had a bandstand built. The whole town had a ball right along Route 202. I did too, for the band was really great that night.

Tommy was exceptional behind the wheel. As a former sprint car and midget racer I got huge kicks from riding with him, though on occasion he took unnecessary risks. He'd be a normal wheel man until, on the way home to Bernardsville, he'd leave Route 22 and head over the mountains. Then it was Formula One time. He'd slide around tight curves at speeds high enough to put him in a confrontation with any vehicle coming the other way.

That happened one Monday morning. Tommy had an early important meeting with an executive at MCA. I had to be in my *Variety* office early, too. We left the estate at about 7:30. Tommy gunned his '38 Buick convertible around those curves until he roared around one and slid to the other side of the road. A small pickup was headed the other way and we got back to where we belonged by inches. It scared hell out of me and Egan. It even shook Tommy somewhat.

However, I was with him one winter morning when he really showed me his ability. We came over the top of a hill and hit a long stretch of slick ice on a down grade, with a curve at the bottom. We were moving at high speed and how he kept that car straight while braking on ice and yet slowed enough to get around the bend in one piece, I'll never know. The man was a master.

As I've said, Tommy and I frequently clashed. Perhaps the worst erupted one year when I was assigned to review his stage show at New York's Paramount Theater. This was the band that had Buddy Rich on drums, fourteen strings, Sinatra, Jo Stafford, the Pied Pipers, all atop eight brass, five sax, and rhythm--about thirty people in all.

The fourteen strings came about when Phil Braunstein, T.D.'S accountant, advised him that his federal taxes were such that it would actually cost only $200 a week to add them. By doing so, T.D. increased his theater salary to about $15,000 weekly, big money for those years. Of course, by presenting such an entourage, Tommy forced other leaders on the same level to increase personnel, mostly via strings, in order to compete.

Onstage, during one of the band's main numbers, Ziggy Elman was standing in a spotlight making that trumpet talk as only he and a few others could. Buddy Rich slowly dropped the tempo until the band stopped completely. Ziggy had a wad of gum in his mouth (or so it appeared from the audience), which didn't add to his comfort. He took it out and handed it to Rich, who put it in his kisser.

There was a distinct lull. The jam-packed audience sat transfixed trying to figure out what was going on. Tommy stood up front laughing.

While writing the review I began to get annoyed at the effrontery of the two musicians and Tommy. I wrote a separate story castigating Tommy for horsing around while he was supposed to be putting on a professional show for the money he was drawing. Bob Landry, then editing my copy, set the item up as an editorial, which floored me when I saw it in proof.

The editorial hit the music biz like a bomb. The industry buzzed. I was criticized for being too picky. But Bob Weitman, manager of the Paramount, called to say he agreed with me.

Tommy never said boo. About six months later he opened at the Cafe Rouge of the old Pennsylvania Hotel and I was assigned to review. I was a bit leery. Tommy Valando and I went together. We were in the doorway. The band was on the stand. Tommy was nowhere in sight. Suddenly I was upended—literally stood on my head—held by someone very strong. It was Tommy. He'd sneaked up behind us. He was laughing.

Everything was cool again.

That same show at the Paramount featured Red Skelton. He was then just a vaudeville act, albeit one of the funniest. What T.D.'s men did to the guy was unbelievable. Red did a crazy bit called "Guzzler's Gin," which with his "Doughnut Dunking" routine made up an act so funny that the first time I saw it I wound up stuffing a hankerchief in my mouth. Red was a teetotaler and Dorsey's guys knew it. They filled his stage bottle with real gin. The first mouthful he swigged was blown all over the first ten rows of patrons. They did it again a few days later, using liquid not quite as tasty.

I think one of the best stories remotely involving T.D. concerned Lorraine and me. Tommy had been telling me about a new Sy Oliver arrangement of a thing called "Opus One," which he'd already rehearsed in preparation for recording for RCA-Victor.

One night a couple weeks later Lorraine and I, still newlyweds, were playing in the sack. We had a T.D. broadcast on the bedside radio. Without warning the band hit the opening of "Opus." It caught my ear and I raised my head. Consequently, I forgot what I was doing and things went "pffft", as Walter Winchell would say.

Tommy had a tremendous arrangement of "Sunny Side of the Street," which opened with a drum and brass crash. He used it often to wake up the crowd when the band returned from intermission. One night at the Cafe Rouge I was sitting next to the bandstand prattling away to a friend and actually tipped my chair over backward and hit the floor, it startled me so. Tommy chortled like a maniac.

Tommy took his band away from the Paramount Theater one year, playing instead the huge Capitol Theater, farther up Broadway. I visited backstage after reviewing the show. The first thing he threw at me was, "What do you think I bought last night?" Then he showed me a picture of a 33-foot Chris-Craft cabin cruiser he'd picked up on a casual visit to the New York Boat Show.

The boat cost him exactly $1,000-a-foot. A year or so later Pat and a pilot brought it to Florida, where the band was working. On a cruise on Biscayne Bay Tommy saw Walter P. Chrysler's 96-foot yacht. He had to have it. He told me later he swapped the 33-footer for the 96-footer, and threw in $90,000. The bigger job required a crew.

After the advent of the big yacht, Tommy acquired a land-cruiser—a bus outfitted with all the comforts of home. It was a great rig and Tommy got his kicks driving it. One summer Tommy was playing the Steel Pier in Atlantic City. Lorraine and I went to see him. He was ensconced in a suite at the Haddon Hall, across from the Pier (now Resorts International).

I said to him, "Where's the boat?"

"Out in the bay," he answered.

I came back with, "Where's the cruiser?"

"Down in the parking lot," he rejoined.

"What's with the suite?" I wanted to know.

"I need a base nearby," he answered.

That was Tommy Dorsey.

Probably the last time I talked seriously with Tommy was in the summer of 1950, after I had left *Variety* to co-manage the Ralph Flanagan Orchestra. He called to suggest we have a drink. When we met he wasted no time telling me he objected to my early methods in selling the Flanagan band to ballroom operators. He said I was undermining the asking prices of the older, more established bands. At that point he and other top outfits were asking guarantees of $2,500 a night during the week and higher weekends.

I had set the one-night ballroom price for Flanagan, then the hottest property in the business, at $1,000 a night, $1,500 weekends.

When Herb Hendler and I started the Flanagan orchestra the band was a hit on RCA-Victor records. A big hit. But I still was not certain of the band's real box-office draw, considering the declining condition of the band biz. If I priced the band too high and it did not justify the cost to a promoter, we could go one-time around, then forget the whole thing and look for another way to make a living. However, at $1,000 a night, if we did as well as record sales indicated we might and went into percentage (the magic words to ballroom men) we'd earn the equal of a high guarantee anyway. Thus, we might have a salable property with a long-time earning capacity.

I pointed out to Tommy that I had not left my cushy spot as Music Editor of a world-circulated paper to manage a "once-around the circuit" orchestra. So, I had set Flanagan's price to promoters at $1,000 a night. That way we would make money over and above the guarantee and the promoters would make money and everybody would be happy.

As nicely and as friendly as I could, I told Tommy frankly that I was not worried about his band or anyone else's. I was concerned only with Flanagan's future for my financial sake, and if Dorsey took a dim view of our operation it was just one of those things. Tommy was unmoved. He didn't like it and told me so in no uncertain terms.

At the end of our first string of one-nighters we took a back-page ad in *Variety* to tell the music world that the Ralph Flanagan Orchestra went into percentage on every single one of 60-odd one-nighters.

I didn't see much of Tommy over the next few years, between the management business and my growing family. So whatever breach had occurred wasn't repaired.

I was in California when I learned of his death and could not get back in time for the services.

I was sorry because Tommy was a valued friend and a great name in the overall scheme of the big band era.

And his death was so unnecessary. Living in Westchester County, above New York City, he'd had an Italian meal sent up from his favorite restaurant. Apparently he indulged himself heavily, then took sleeping pills and went to bed early in preparation for an early rise for an appointment in the city. During the night, lying on his back, he became nauseated, heaved, didn't awaken because of the pills, and drowned. A terrible and ignominious end to a great musician, bandleader, and "Era" personality.

There was none other like him in the music business of the time.

CHAPTER 5

Jimmy Dorsey

For some years after the battle at the Astor and their later resumption of brotherly love, Tommy and Jimmy remained on good terms. I was in a position to observe both closely and got frequent reports from Jimmy's manager, Billy Burton.

The aftermath of the Astor imbroglio drew me closer to Tommy, a position I could not reach with Jimmy.

Jimmy was not as conscious as Tommy about promoting himself or his band. He had a press-agent, as did all the big bands. He also had personal manager Burton, who was as good as any p.a. at promoting Jimmy—and himself. As a consequence Jimmy paid little attention to press people. He'd answer questions when necessary, but that was not his bag.

Jimmy liked my accompanying him and Burton on one-night dates fairly close to New York, which I did often because it provided me with experience both for my job and, as it later turned out, in managing bands and artists. But, I frequently kidded, he liked me along only because of my fast, light touch on the wheel and brakes of his Cadillac, which enabled him to sleep like a baby all the way home from wherever the band played (Burton didn't drive).

Jimmy was not nearly as blatant as Tommy about sex. Instead, he reached the same goals by being sneaky fast rather than openly aggressive.

Jimmy was a musician's musician. Leaders who had been sidemen in radio studio bands, as most prominent leaders once were, usually had strong rapport with their men, which sometimes led to an unwillingness to discipline, which frequently led to a sloppy band. Such was not a Jimmy Dorsey problem. He led an excellent combination after Tommy's defection, which meandered along at a comfortable rate of earning power, until early in 1941.

I'm certain it was 1941 because at about 10 P.M. on January 22 Lorraine went into labor with our first son. I drove her to the hospital and found the facility didn't have a waiting room for expectant fathers. At loose, nervous ends, I called Burton at the Pennsylvania Hotel, where Jimmy was working the Cafe Rouge. He suggested I come to the hotel, said the band was going to rehearse new tunes after closing. "We can keep calling the hospital," he said, to "let them know where you are."

At 5 A.M. we went to his apartment. I called the hospital and left the phone number of where I was, which turned out to be like talking down a well. At 10 A.M. the phone rang. It was my mother-in-law. First son William had been born at 6:10 A.M. and the change of hospital staffs left my phone number in the waste basket.

The new songs Jimmy rehearsed were "Amapola" and "Green Eyes," Those two tunes were the catalysts which projected the

Jimmy Dorsey Orchestra into the upper regions of popularity and earnings. They were followed by additional smashes— "Tangerine," "My Prayer," and "White Cliffs of Dover," written by Burton's brother, Nat, a professional songwriter.

After I quit *Variety* to go into management I had little connection with either Bill Burton or Jimmy. They split before Jimmy went back into an alliance with brother Tommy in a renewal of the original Dorsey Brothers Orchestra, which did very well as part of a summer replacement show for Jackie Gleason's highly-rated TV program.

After Tommy's death Jimmy began drinking much more heavily than usual, very likely because he knew of the cancer that eventually took his life. (The two brothers died within six or seven months of each other.)

As for Burton, who I thought was a real friend rather than just another guy looking for a break in *Variety's* music pages, the man turned out like so many others. He revealed his true colors when I managed a group called The Beachcombers. Their story appears in another chapter.

To get back to Jimmy, even though he had cancer he continued to work--and drink heavily. The band was booked into the Orpheum Theater, Minneapolis. As one of his musicians later described the scene to me, Jimmy was on stage having a terrible time playing his sax solos because he was drunk. He was being booed. Finally, a voice from the balcony asked, "Why don't you sober up, ya drunk?"

Jimmy retorted, "Fuck You, Mac."

Down came the curtain, sadly and prophetically.

CHAPTER 6

Artie Shaw

Artie Shaw's clarinet was the equal in some ways to Benny Goodman's great talent. He was an extremely exciting newcomer when his recording of "Begin the Beguine" hit big in the 1930's.

The Artie Shaw Orchestra became as near to #1 as could be— and then faded because of the deliberate defection of its leader.

One evening Shaw did what many bandleaders of the Big Band Era would like to have done, if they were struggling. He stepped off the bandstand of the Cafe Rouge at the Pennsylvania Hotel and disappeared. But the difference between Shaw and other bandleaders was that the band he deserted was highly successful rather than struggling. "Begin the Beguine" accomplished that.

I got the news of Shaw's Thursday defection from his pressagent and my close friend Kay Hansen when Kay and his wife picked up Lorraine and me on the following Saturday evening. We went to dinner, then drove down the New Jersey coast to listen to Jack Teagarden's new band.

I checked on Monday with Andrew Weinberger, Shaw's attorney, and found that Artie had not yet contacted him. I wrote the story for Tuesday's *Variety* deadline and was amazed to find that Shaw's action was still not generally known. (*Billboard* went to press on Friday and *Downbeat* and *Metronome* weren't weeklies.)

It appeared we were going to have a clean break on what in those days was big news. A top-name bandleader deserting a financially successful band?. Ridiculous.

But there was a hitch in my "scoop." On the *Variety* staff as a proofreader, assistant to the famed Epes Sergeant, was a youngster named George Gilbert, whose father was a *New York World-Telegram* reporter. The kid had seen my story in proof. As we were putting *Variety* "to bed" on Tuesday afternoon I overheard this stupid youngster reading my Shaw story to someone on the phone. He was talking to his father. The *World-Telly* featured the story on the front page of its final edition and *Variety's* "scoop," to use a hated word, went down the drain.

I should have advised Abel Green, Managing Editor, what had occurred. I don't know why I didn't except that the damage had already been done. Abel would have fired the kid forthwith. Revealing a paper's content before publication is a no-no of the first water.

What made the whole thing worse was that *Variety* didn't hit the newsstands until the following morning and it appeared that we had picked up the story from the *World-Telly*.

Shaw went to Mexico for a vacation and while there found some great songs, which, when he finally returned to New York, were turned into smash hits for RCA-Victor. The best was "Frenesi," backed by "Adios Mariquita Linda," both made with a string section. He recorded another huge hit with the same setup, a great arrangement of "I Cover the Waterfront."

Meanwhile, Tony Pastor had taken over leadership of the Shaw "Begin the Beguine" combination and went on about his business under the management of Joe Shribman and ex-trumpeter Charlie Trotta. They acquired the Clooney Sisters from a Cincinnati radio station and the band did very well financially.

Eventually the band moved to Columbia Records and one of the songs it recorded there launched Rosemary Clooney on her way to the top. Titled "Grievin' for You," it was cut at such a low sound level that coin machine operators couldn't use it since it could not be heard clearly.

My review of the disk, a rave, caused Manie Sachs to sign Rosemary to a separate Columbia contract. Then, after Mitch Miller took over the Artists and Repertoire (A&R) post from Sachs, he gave her songs that kicked her career into high-gear ("Come on-a My House," etc.)

Shaw made his initial and heaviest impact on the band business from a Boston ballroom, aided by Sy Shribman, an operator who had financial hooks into the beginnings of a number of big bands, including Glenn Miller. He had several ballrooms, one in Taunton, Massachusetts, that was a big earner because it was situated between Boston and Providence. Shaw's radio broadcasts from Boston backed up his "Begin the Beguine" record smash and he began making big box office noises.

In the summer of 1938 Martin Block, WNEW, New York's pre-eminent disk jockey, ran a big band bash at Randall's Island that covered the entire day. The Island's huge playing field was jammed—no charge.

Block had such power in the New York market that he was able to induce ten or twelve of the hottest bands to the Island's bandstand. One of the brightest of the stars he conned into coming was Shaw. Artie brought his band down from Boston just for the soiree and I clearly recall the excitement attending his arrival, caused by Block's repeated announcements of Shaw's road progress by bus toward the stadium. Shaw was restless, apparently not the kind of guy to lead a successful Big Band. He hated the fans, one of the major reasons for his later defection. He simply could not abide the discomfort of catering to the kids who paid the freight. He made that clear very often. But he tried hard, it seemed to me, to change.

After his return from Mexico and the record successes beginning with "Frenesi," he put a band together for a string of one-nighters. With Howard Sinnott, one-night booker for General Artists Corporation (GAC), I drove to Pennsylvania to attend one. Artie, Howard, and I were talking outside during an intermission when a youngster walked up and asked Artie to slip him past the doorman. Instead Artie slipped him the price of admission. I couldn't fathom whether the move was for my benefit or Artie was mellowing.

In 1942 Shaw was induced to join the Navy—not to see the world, but to form a band for the entertainment of servicemen. He coaxed a number of musician friends (who might eventually have been drafted anyhow) into joining up. One of them was Dick Jones, an arranger with whom I was later associated at Capitol Records. The stories Jones tells about Shaw's hitch and his eventual discharge could fill a separate book.

It must be noted, that Shaw's service outfit went into active wartime areas and withstood many a Japanese bombing run, which did the nerves of guys accustomed to blowing horns rather than being blown up little good. Especially Shaw's, according to the rundown Jones gave me.

But, his treatment of the men he induced to join up with him and then "deserted," which they felt he did when he took an early discharge, made most of the guys in that band anti-Shaw then and for years afterward.

Before Shaw was released from the navy, but after it became known that he would be, the band was traveling by Navy destroyer from one base to another. Shaw, according to Jones, liked to stand on the fantail of a moving ship at night if the weather permitted. Such was their attitude toward him at that point, Dick claimed, that several of his musicians plotted to sneak up behind him, lift him by the ankles, and toss him overboard. Obviously, they were only kidding, or, at the least, lost their nerve.

Likable or not, however, there's no question Artie Shaw contributed heavily to the Big band era, musically and promotionally.

Shaw was married seven times: to Margaret Allen, Lana Turner, Elizabeth Kern, Ava Gardner, Kathleen Windsor, Doris Dowling, and Evelyn Keyes. Maybe some of his puzzling career moves and defections came from his courtships and troubled marriages and fathering two sons and divorce after divorce after divorce—all involving some of the most glamorous women in the world. Maybe you could just chalk it up to a searching, restless spirit.

CHAPTER 7

Woody Herman

There were so many great bands during the "Era" that it is extremely difficult to line them up in order of popularity. However, Woody Herman's "Third Herd" belonged in the upper echelon. It was one of the most exciting combinations of all time.

Woody was one leader for whom I had a great deal of respect and liking. I visited him as often as possible. One of the best times was in early 1942, when I was invited by him on a flight across country. The trip was a dilly.

The "Flying Fortress" revved its engines and moved down the runway. I was standing in the narrow track above the bomb bay doors, holding onto overhead girders. Next to me were saxist Flip Phillips and pianist/arranger, Ralph Burns. We were scared stiff. There were high wires at the runway end and there was no certainty we would clear them. Luckily, we made it.

The bomber was heavily overloaded—not with bombs, but with the members of Woody's band, plus their instruments and baggage.

The airport was at Jacksonville, Michigan, and we were headed for Air Force bases at Clovis and Roswell, New Mexico. Woody's nightly money guarantee was by then up to $2,500, so his managers had made a deal to play two dates for the Air Force at $1,000 a crack in exchange for being flown to Hollywood, where the band was to open for the first time at the Palladium Ballroom.

Commercial flying was impossible. Moving across country by train was difficult. Movement by bus was equally hard in view of fuel rationing. So, the Air Force deal was a godsend.

Woody invited me along. I'd never been to the West Coast. I hated to leave Lorraine and our young son, Bill, but she felt I should go and so did my boss Abel Green, who looked upon the trip as "seasoning."

I'm sure Woody offered me the trip as a "thank you" for the attention I had given the band when it was struggling.

The first time I heard of the Woody Herman Orchestra, I was still a "cub," but learning the band business fast. When I heard something I liked, I didn't hesitate to broadcast it to the world, by printed word and mouth. That's what happened with Woodrow.

I was assigned to review a show at the Brooklyn Strand Theater, featuring the then obscure Ozzie Nelson Orchestra, vocals by Harriet Hilliard. Juggy Gayles, an aspiring "songplugger" and new friend, asked to go with me. It was the Friday before Christmas and snowing heavily. As we exited the theater, Juggy suggested we go to the nearby Roseland Ballroom, operated by the same people as the New York Roseland. There was a band there he wanted me to hear. I wanted to get home. Juggy pleaded.

Woody Herman's "Blue Flames" Orchestra was the attraction. He was despondent. There were more musicians than patrons in the ballroom (understandable given the date and weather) and he was thinking of disbanding. He felt the band was going nowhere, that his booking agency (GAC) was derelict, and Decca Records, for which he had already recorded some sides, was giving him short-shrift. The sides had not yet been scheduled for release. And Roseland was not exactly a prize booking. It featured local radio station (WHN) broadcasts, which was like blowing into the Holland Tunnel.

The reason for working most "location" dates at that time was primarily for the promotional benefit provided by the network broadcast wires (NBC Red and Blue nets, CBS and WOR, New York). All did big band "remotes" every night following the 11 p.m. news. WOR, an independent, offered the widest national coverage via a network of independent stations across the country. In contrast, WHN covered a 50-mile radius.

I flipped over the band. I shouted loud and long. I wrote what probably is to this day the longest review of a band ever printed by *Variety*. I got after my friends Tom Rockwell and Mike Nidorf at GAC and they got off their keisters, if only to take advantage of what I stirred up. Decca came around. It released "Woodchopper's Ball" and "Blues on Parade," the former still one of the band's best. GAC booked the band into the Famous Door, New York and the spot reprinted my review on an easel outside the entrance on opening night. In a matter of weeks the band began to gather steam.

Woodrow never looked back. His WHN days were over. It was network time.

The band, of course, changed over the years. I rate the "Third Herd" as one of the most exciting bands of all time. "Caldonia" and "Happiness Is a Thing Called Joe" are among my most-played recordings.

To get back to our cross-country flight—originally, five "Flying Fortresses" were sent to pick us up. (For me to meet him, Woody provided me with sleeping accommodations on the New York Central's Wolverine, the first time I rode a fast train.) Only two planes arrived, which was why we were strapped on takeoff. One plane had engine trouble, another landed in Iowa and got mired in mud (the pilot wanted to visit his girl friend), and the third just got lost.

When we got to the Jacksonville airport that morning, the Air Corps Major in charge took one look at the entourage and equipment and unequivocally stated that at least half would have to go by train. Since we were due to play at Clovis, New Mexico, that very night it was obvious that smarts he didn't have. When the two pilots finished arguing we were packed aboard the two planes to face the risky takeoffs.

We had a ball the entire trip—with just one sour note. Before the dance at Jacksonville, Davey Tough, one of the greatest drummers in band biz history, but a heavy drinker, had turned up missing. We scoured the town with no luck. Woody finally used a local substitute, but the band was not the same. Davey was found in bed the next morning, sobered up.

At Clovis the band was quartered in a Quonset hut. Woody and I sat facing a long corridor down the center. Davey entered the far end and appeared headed for Woody's quarters. He stopped, stepped back, and entered a room we knew was not his. He emerged fifteen minutes later falling-down drunk. (In that time he had drained what was left of a bottle of rye in Ralph Burns' room.) It was the fastest transition I ever witnessed. The next morning, he was stretchered aboard the plane for Roswell and hospitalized, then stretchered aboard again for the final trip to Hollywood. He never again played with Woody. (Don Lamont, almost as great, replaced him.)

Leaving Clovis, our now three planes were parked near a group of roped-off, very large aircraft, each protected by an armed guard. They were B-29's on their way to Saipan. One eventually dropped the A-bomb.

On the way west we had fun. The pilots simulated "battle formation," which meant flying with wing-tips almost touching. It scared "Popsie," then Woody's band-boy, into asking, "Where did you get your wings—in Woolworth's?"

We flew at about 3,500 feet. If a hill 3,000 feet or so came up, the pilots didn't lift; we'd cross 500 feet above the hilltop, often scattering herds of deer. Neal Reid, a former member of the band, already in the Army and returning to base, was with us. He and I occupied the "Green House," the bombardier's "office" in the nose of the plane. So, we saw everything.

It was a weird experience to sit out on the bombardier's stool, surrounded by plexiglass. It gave one the feeling of flying alone. It was even weirder to land that way. During the initial part of the flight from Jacksonville, our pilots were advised that one of the missing three planes would meet us at Oklahoma City, to siphon some of our load. On landing, all personnel are banned from the "Green House," because if the ship flips, the first thing crushed is the nose. But they forgot we were down there; I believe it was then my hair got curlier.

Perhaps the funniest thing during the entire trip was when the navigator, a trainer who'd been busy with slide rule and wind drift equipment, suddenly looked up and said, "According to my reckoning, Phoenix should be dead ahead. I don't see it anywhere." (It was ten miles south.) I was thankful we weren't on a flight to Guam.

Reaching the Hollywood area, Woody and I donned earphones connected to the pilot's radio. The Van Nuys airport was heavily camouflaged. Nothing could be seen from the air. It was a sea of green. Our pilots were completely lost. We'd hear the controllers below saying, "You're right above us, look sharp."

I was apprehensive since I'd heard the pilot order the other two planes to circle and the Hollywood haze was already beginning to manifest itself; I didn't know that when circling in the same area, it's done at different altitudes.

Finally a controller advised us that a commercial plane was approaching. "Find him, get on his tail and come on in," he advised. Both Woody and I saw the plane. So did the pilot. Before we could close he disappeared as though a genie went "poof." Another plane, another "poof." Finally, we got on another's tail, the others lined up behind, and we all dropped onto the runway.

Exiting the aircraft, I went speechless. There was a rope canopy above us that must have been a half-mile long, impregnated with tree branches, so it seemed. Under it were at least 25 Constellations, a newly developed Air Force entry. From above not a thing could be seen.

Woody put me up at a Hollywood hotel. He and his wife, Charlotte, stayed at the Garden of Allah, where most visiting bandleaders lived. (It is now, and has been for some time, a gay gathering place.) Charlotte was one of the most attractive red-haired women I have ever met and as gracious as could be.

I spent ten days in Hollywood, royally entertained by Arthur Ungar, publisher of *Daily Variety* and then one of most powerful men in the film capital. He and his wife saw to my "seasoning" in grand manner. They dined me at Chasen's, Romanoff's and other gossip-column watering holes of Hollywood's top echelon.

Woody had arranged for me to go home on the Santa Fe Chief, one of the nation's fastest and most luxurious trains. It was my first trip across country by land and I was knocked out by the Rockies and the other sights. For a New Yorker born in an East 42d Street tenement, the West was some wallop.

The rest of Woody's history is, as they say, history. Almost until his death in 1989, Woody managed to stay near the top of what was left of the Big Band Era.

It was a sad day for me when I first read about Woodrow's ill health. Charlotte had died relatively young, which for him compounded financial problems caused by repeated poor choices in personal managers. Between the Roseland Ballroom and the Famous Door date, which springboarded him, songwriter Sammy Cahn and Juggy Gayles had aligned Woody with a manager/attorney firm to which he gave power-of-attorney. There were problems some years later, after which the alliance was dissolved.

Woody then took on a manager who was the epitome of the "I'll Tell You What I'm Gonna Do" pitchman who did the commercials on Milton Berle's old TV show. This guy would sell you at any given moment one of a dozen watches, diamond rings, necklaces, etc., which he had on his person at all times. I suspect he was with the band because he helped keep it financially afloat.

Both alliances had to contribute to the problems so widely publicized prior to Woody's death. He owned a house in the Hollywood Hills (hanging from a cliff), which I visited several times. That should have been a legacy to his daughter instead of being sacrificed because he had been taken advantage of earlier.

Woody did not throw money around like so many other Big Band Era leaders and should have closed his life with a fair fortune.

Woody Herman was a nice man. Too nice, perhaps.

CHAPTER 8

Sammy Kaye

Sweet bands of the "Era" often were led by singers or instrumentalists who could not approach, talent-wise, the big stars of the time. Bands in this category usually were led by men content with their standing and relatively low earning capacity because they were not aggressive enough.

Sammy Kaye did not fit that mold. He was thinking every minute. And he drove his band from obscurity to national prominence, with the help of his Manager Jim Peppe. Kaye was the type of personality you would hug one minute and kill the next. I had more fun watching him operate than any other bandleader I knew.

Sammy had the guts of a burglar to go with three priorities in his life:

1. To lead a successful orchestra.
2. To play golf as often as possible and well.
3. To screw every female he could.

He succeeded on all counts.

Sammy was a giant among lady-killers even though by no means close to a mental picture of Don Juan. He was short, slight, and wore a toupee that had a disturbing habit of becoming unglued at the rarest times.

Out of Sam's persistent striving after anything in skirts came some hilarious stories. Most stemmed from his highly successful gimmick "So You Want to Lead a Band," which he developed into a very profitable feature. It was a simple routine based on the fact that in every audience there are exhibitionists who will do almost anything to get into the spotlight. Staple vaudeville acts over the years were based on that premise, but where these acts got laughs by making fools of audience-participants, Sammy simply let them make fools of themselves. He handed them batons and let them conduct his orchestra. The musicians followed every little movement of the baton, and some weird and funny sounds resulted. Laughs came by the ton.

The beauty of the bit was that it could be done anywhere—in a ballroom, theater, nightclub, on radio, and on TV because the sound of the band stumbling along under an erratic wand-waver was sufficiently funny.

Over the years, Sam snagged a comfortable covey of conquests via the gimmick. One of the most amusing I witnessed occurred one Saturday afternoon at the Strand Theater, New York. I stepped into the theater, after a couple of hours of writing at the nearby *Variety* office, to discuss an upcoming golf tournament with Sam—only to find the band was onstage.

I slipped into the audience. Sam had a delicious-looking young woman at the mike. He began his usual questions: her name, hometown, etc. When he asked what she did for a living, the girl hesitated. Sam idly pressed for an answer. Finally, she asked,

"Must I tell you?" Sam said, "Not really, but we'd like to know." By this time the audience was beginning to sense why she was so reluctant. She sotto-voced into Sammy's ear, "I'm a hooker."

Sam smartly played it straight. He came back with a brilliant, "Is that right? How's business?" while the audience broke up.

"Great," was the comeback.

Sam then asked whether it was a good business to be in and the girl cracked back, "If you're young and attractive and if you don't waste your time going to vaudeville shows." At this juncture the audience howled loud and long.

I never did get to Sam at the show's end. He was busy chasing all over the house trying to find the gal. He even had ushers on the lookout. He found her eventually, but for once couldn't score. She brushed him off.

Get a few musicians or music publishers together and inevitably they get around to Mr. Kaye. Ralph Flanagan tells a great story. He was Sam's pianist for several years. The band was on location date at a Minneapolis hotel. One night, after the job, Flanagan and another musician went out on the town. Walking the corridor toward their rooms at 5 a.m., they heard a muffled scream. Suddenly, they were facing a naked gal running toward them. Seeing them, she turned and raced back where she came from, but before she could get inside they saw something in her hand.

The room was Sammy Kaye's and the item in her fist was Sam's rug.

Apparently, Sam was giving the girl a little "head." When she hit the high spots she grabbed him by the hair, not an unnatural move under the circumstances. His toupee came off. The girl didn't know he wore one and got so frightened she leaped out of bed and out of the room in the buff. She thought she had scalped him.

Sam was in Atlanta once for a one-nighter. The dance promoter, knowing Sam's proclivity for pussy, sat in the hotel coffee shop with a young sacrifice in tow, waiting for him to awaken (he'd spent the night on a bus, traveling from the previous date). Impatient to be on his way, the promoter told the girl to go up to Sam's room and surprise him. The girl was back in five minutes.

"What's wrong?" asked the promoter.

"You must have given me the wrong room," the girl snapped, "there's no one in that room but an old bastard with no hair and no teeth and he sure wasn't expecting me."

Sam was smart about his rugs. He had a dozen or more, each cut to different lengths starting with a short one and progressing through succeedingly longer ones to where the whole process started all over. I came across that information after arriving at a Montclair, New Jersey, hotel to pick him up for a golf date with Frank Dailey. Sam was in the shower. He shouted for me to come in. I did and almost fell down when I was greeted by a dozen or more dome doilies, each on its own skull, distributed around the room.

Sam's rugs were a constant source of merriment and, to his credit, he joined in the laughs. Like the night we left the Commodore Hotel in New York at 2 a.m. with a couple of music publishers for a quick snack at Lindy's. It was winter and blowing. Sam stepped out the door and his hat and rug together went flying east while we walked west. It took all four of us to round up his errant locks.

In the spring of 1943 the Kaye band was booked to do a Coca Cola radio broadcast from Camp Endicott, the Naval Base near Providence. Sam invited me along and, though it was my usual day off, a time I always tried to spend with my wife and young son, I was curious and I agreed to join him.

We took a train to Providence; the Navy picked us up and gave our troupe a royal time. It was more than fifty years ago, but two incidents still stand out in my mind. Having been trained in the sanctity of the bathroom, I can still remember the tremendous shock I got when, directed to a Quonset hut when the need arose, I walked into the "Men's Room" and found forty johns facing each other. No dividers—nothing. Which didn't seem to bother two sailors sitting on adjacent thrones playing checkers on a board between them.

Sam's brass with women worked overtime on the way home. The midnight train between Boston and Washington was jammed by the time we boarded. We walked through five or six cars. Suddenly, Sam spotted a smart-looking gal in a corner surrounded by luggage. He sweet-talked her into letting us use two of her valises to sit on, drew her into conversation during which he found she just adored playing gin and had a deck of cards handy. She promptly took the both of us over a few jumps—at a nickel a point.

Sam left the train with her. About six months later I happened to walk into his office at 608 Fifth Avenue, across the way from Saks Fifth Avenue. Covering the mouthpiece he told me he was talking to "Lisa." When I looked blank he explained, "The gal on the train. Don't you remember?"

He was still working out in the sack with her. I didn't blame him. She was quite a dish.

Another train story that circulated among Sam's cronies for quite a while was a doozy, even for him. It's somewhat on the unbelievable side.

During the war, there were occasions when traveling bands were forced to take trains. This time the Kaye band was changing trains in Washington. There was a three-hour layover. His musicians bet him a goodly sum he could not pick up a strange gal and get laid during the interval. He won the bet. (It was Washington, a town noted for its overload of round-heeled chicks.)

I got to know the girl involved. When Sam played New York she'd often fly in for weekends, and she confirmed the story.

Saks Fifth Avenue provided a hilarious period in the lives of Sam and his office staff. Kaye's offices were quite extensive. Two rooms faced Fifth Avenue and four or five ran down the 49th Street side. These last were one floor above and directly opposite Saks' fitting rooms for women's custom-made gowns, lingerie, and girdles.

Someone on the male staff always had an eye peeled for the "peelers of Saks." When a particularly delectable one began shucking her clothes to be fitted for something, a phone signal would go out and all would race for the window with the best line of sight. It made little difference if the rightful occupant was on the phone, busy with a visitor, or otherwise in conference, they'd all barge in to his office.

It was amazing what went on over there. I've seen stripped-to-the-skin exhibitionists stand at the windows with the Venetian blinds pulled all the way up to admit as much light as possible for a fitting, with one leg up on the sill-level radiator, blithely gazing down into the street while Sam and his men practically hung from the window casings across the way. The women could not possibly have been oblivious. And it happened daily.

Sammy was a great sports enthusiast, particularly golf, although he followed football avidly. At one point we were members, together with Perry Como and other music men, at the Paumonak Country Club on Long Island. At our home club and at others all over Long Island, New Jersey, and Westchester Sam and I had some ding-dong battles, always for money.

Sam's ego and his big mouth got him into a dispute one night at Meadowbrook. At a table with music publisher Jack Bregman and songwriter Milt Yager, he and Yager began arguing over some vague golfing point. It ended up with Yager challenging Sam to a $500 Nassau ($500 each nine and $500 over the full 18 holes), the winnings to go to charity. They agreed to play the next day at Glen Oaks, on Long Island, one of the most beautiful courses I've ever played. Both Yager and Bregman were members. Bregman and I were invited to fill out a foursome.

On the third hole, a relatively easy par four, Sam dropped his second shot into a high bunker guarding the green. Then we found that some lunkhead had climbed out of the trap over the top and had left a six-inch deep footprint, which his equally careless caddie hadn't raked. Sam's ball rolled up the slope and nestled deep in the hole, a million-to-one shot.

Sam stood stunned. He could barely see the ball. Yager walked up, took one look and snapped, "Play it, you s.o.b."

Charity or not, Sam hated to lose at anything. By the time he holed out he had a triple bogey and was so livid he chopped up the rest of the course, while Yager chortled his way around. At least the $1,500 was deductible.

Sam and I and three other music publishers were informed sometime in 1950 or 1951 that the Engineers course in Roslyn, Long Island was up for sale. The asking price was $50,000. We immediately formed a combination, each putting up $10,000, and a deposit was offered to the owners. They hesitated, then eventually backed off. In a few years the land alone was worth millions.

Sam was married just once, to a loaded Shaker Heights, Ohio, matron who had one son. Since the wedding occurred during the early days of the war there were those who suggested that ol' Sam was dodging the draft. Perhaps that was true. It was none of my business. As far as I was concerned Sam was Sam. I got a kick out of him.

As a matter of fact, when the war started I was 29, married with one son, and I was a newspaperman. Whether I was exempted by the son, the marriage, or the newspaper position, I never determined. I weighed then a slim 123 pounds, and would have gone if drafted.

At any rate, Sam's marriage was what today might be called "open," at least from his viewpoint. He never stopped chasing pussy and Ruth didn't ever seem to run out of patience with him. There was one time, however, when his staff blew it. They always protected his keister, but this time they slipped up and could do nothing but stand by and wait for the lid to blow.

Again it happened at the Strand Theater, on Broadway, the Warner Bros. flagship. I stumbled into it simply by walking through the stage door a minute behind Mrs. Kaye. Sam's road manager, bandboy, and an executive from his office were running around like madmen. They didn't know where to hide. It seemed that Ruth had gotten past all of them, including the stage door guard, and was climbing the stairs to Sam's dressing room by the time she was spotted. She opened the door, to be greeted by Sam's skinny fanny rhythmically bouncing over a lovely blonde.

Mrs. Kaye quietly eased the door shut, came back downstairs without a word, and left the theater without a glance at anyone.

Ask almost anyone old enough and they'll tell where they were on Pearl Harbor Sunday. Sam and I were together at New York's Polo Grounds watching the Giants vs. the Brooklyn Dodgers football teams. The Kaye band that fall was doing a 30-minute broadcast on NBC radio 1:00 to 1.30 p.m. every Sunday, a show that included Sam's poetry gimmick. I would drive in and park near the 50th Street entrance to the RCA Building, from which the program originated. Listening to the show, I would have the car running and in gear when Sam popped through the door. We would get to the park in the middle of the first quarter.

During the week prior to the game Sam handed me a ticket, telling me the game was too important to miss any part, and he'd take a cab after the broadcast.

When I saw him coming he had a funny look on his face. The second he sat down he whispered, "The Japs bombed Pearl Harbor and all hell is breaking loose." A few minutes later fans in the jammed park, who had no way of knowing what was going down unless they had radios, started looking at one another when the stadium's p.a. system began advising newspaper executives, Army and Navy high-ranking officers, etc., to call their offices, or "report to your cars," as I clearly recall the paging of the *New York Daily News* publisher.

I remember Jimmy Dorsey's Orchestra was at Meadowbrook and when I drove home after dropping Sam, the band was doing a one-hour afternoon radio remote from the club. During the entire hour I think Jimmy got less than two full arrangements on the air. Every few seconds there'd be a fresh news bulletin.

Sam's NBC broadcast, titled "Sunday Serenade," featured one of the money-making "hooks" that helped make the Kaye orchestra a national name, and Sammy a very rich man. On the broadcast he read poetry. Music biz people ragged him unmercifully about it; to watch him get into the mood to deliver was like watching a Shakespearean actor preparing his role.

Sam almost swallowed the mike as he literally breathed the lines.

The kidding didn't bother Sam one whit. He knew what he was doing. He was aware that there were legions of amateur poets out there and he invited them to send him their creations for evaluation and possible broadcast. Entries came in by the ton. Of course, a listener who sent him a poem automatically gave up title.

As usual, ol' Sam had the last laugh on his critics. After a number of weeks on the air, I walked into his offices one day to see a huge table piled high with slips of paper, each with dollar bills attached. Sam had put a number of his broadcast poems into a hardcover book and advertised them at $1 each. That was another minor fortune.

Sammy had a weird sense of humor. One night a few weeks before I was married late in 1939, my fiancée and I went into the city to see a Broadway show. Afterward we went to the Commodore Hotel, where the band was working the Century Room. It was late and few patrons were in the room, so Sam spent a great deal of time with us. Suddenly he turned to me and, in a very low voice, said, "By the way, Bern, what do you do with your wife when you go out nights like this?" I fell on the floor when I saw the look on Lorraine's face. It took me several days to convince her that I was not married and hadn't been. Sammy chortled about my discomfiture for weeks.

Later in his career, when the band was solidly established, Sam was signed for the Roof Garden at the Astor Hotel, on Times Square. I was assigned to review. Abel asked that I pay particular attention to a trio that would be playing between Kaye's sets (such groups often were looked upon as "fill-ins" and disregarded).

I found the trio a fantastic combination and devoted almost all the review to its performance, giving Sammy's band, which I had reviewed often, about fifteen lines in the last paragraph. Sam was furious, but he never cracked until months later. It perhaps was an uncalled-for slap, but it got me off the nut for the many shots he had given me in the past.

For example, once after finishing a round of golf. It didn't happen often, but this time I owed Sam money. I came up with all but a quarter because I couldn't get change. Some time later, I reviewed the band at the Strand Theater in Brooklyn. After the show, I went backstage, to find Sam just off the wings talking to some top MCA executives, his bookers. When he saw me approaching he sang out, "Where's that quarter you still owe me?" The agency guys looked at me like a deadbeat. I slowly reached into my pocket and came up with a half-dollar. I tossed it at him and said, "I still don't have change, but here's your quarter with a quarter interest," turned on my heel and walked. He chased me all the way to the subway trying to induce me to cab it back to Manhattan with him.

"No way," I said. We didn't talk for weeks.

Sam got into band leading by forming a group while at Ohio University in Athens. After graduation he sought to continue and approached a man named Jim Peppe (brother of Lou Peppe, the renowned Ohio State swimming coach), then with Columbia Artists, an important booking agency of the time. Jim went all out to build the Sammy Kaye Orchestra into a national name. Obviously, he succeeded beyond all expectations. To understand what a task it was and to what extent Sammy and his mentor were successful, look back at the popularity ratings of dozens of big bands of the era and, with the exception of Guy Lombardo, there was not a "sweet band" of any importance. They all were second-level, so to speak.

Eventually, the band began making noise. Signed to RCA-Victor, one of the first big hits it recorded was an unusual version of "Daddy," a song from a Pennsylvania University "Mask and Wig" production. In the meantime, Sam and Jim were busy dreaming up gimmicks such as the "So You Want to Lead a Band" bit and the poetry. In a relatively short time the band was one of the best money-makers in the country. And it continued to be a valuable asset to Sam long after the band business faded from the main scene.

I retired in 1979 and moved to Fort Lauderdale. Reading the paper one night after dinner, Lorraine saw an ad indicating Sam would be working that weekend at the Galt Ocean Mile Hotel. We decided to go and bug ol' Sam.

We went to the Friday night opening. I didn't let Sam know I was in the room. Dancing past the bandstand the second time around I slyly glanced up at Sam in time to see him studying the two of us. I gave no indication of anything. I hadn't seen him in several years, my hair was as white as could be and I wore glasses. He continued to study us. Suddenly, when we were ten feet past him and whirling away, he sang out, "Woods, you Irish no-good, come back here!" We had a great weekend.

I saw Sam a few times after that. Once when he came to Fort Lauderdale to play in the Inverarry Golf Tournament as a celebrity guest and once in New York.

I was deeply saddened when he packed it all in in 1989.

He was a great character.

CHAPTER 9

"Sweet" and "Jazz"

Sammy Kaye had media problems in addition to the occasional whack I delivered. They were provided by the big band fan sheets—*Metronome* and *Downbeat.* Unlike musically uneducated me, these people seemingly were steeped in "jazz" music. Their attitude gave the solid impression that they had a corner on that market—that no one else reacted to so-called jazz the way they appreciated that style.

And they hated "sweet bands." They never lost an opportunity to crack down on the performances of Guy Lombardo, Blue Barron, Sammy Kaye or their likes.

George Simon, formerly of *Metronome,* openly made his feelings known on the kind of music Kaye and his compadres delivered in the foreword of his great book on the Big Band Era. He said, "This attitude or preference, or bias (on my part) or whatever you want to call it...my enthusiasm and respect for the less musical bands, no matter how successful they were, have grown not at all."

Though I disagreed, I respect Simon's attitude for that was the way he felt. However, the fallacy in his stance is that it changes when circumstances demand.

George was enlisted in 1993 by *Reader's Digest* to write individual record synopses for its "Big Band Memories" set, offered to subscribers. His comments on Kaye's way-back hit, "It Isn't Fair" goes thusly: "Here the band assays a different approach: rich, full-bodied ensemble sounds with few gimmicks...good music with extremely effective use of dynamics."

Actually, the recording is exactly the sort of thing that Simon sneered at during his *Metronome* days.

In the same pamphlet, Simon comments on Kaye's recording of "Roses" and gets back on track in a nicely disguised choice of words to satisfy those who paid his bill. He says, "Sammy, who liked to keep his music uncomplicated so that everyone could understand it, was often drawn to the simple melodies and harmonies of country music."

The comments on Kaye, and other gentler ones on sweet bands in the *Digest* package, are as far afield from Simon's *Metronome* criticisms of sweet bands as Glenn Miller's style was from Duke Ellington's.

Writing for *Reader's Digest* is quite different.

I feel that by their stances these writers did a disservice to the overall Big Band era. And Simon is still doing it with that short, castigating reference in his otherwise well-written tome. It is a book, by the way, that gives the reader the impression that some of the top bandleaders, such as Tommy Dorsey and Glenn Miller, didn't hire a replacement musician without consulting George. I was as close to Tommy Dorsey as one could get until I left *Variety* and I never once heard Tommy mention Simon's name. At the time of the Era, the top man on *Metronome* was Barry Ulanov.

None of the above is intended as a swipe at Simon. His book is a tremendous job of research and consultations with prominent promotion men of the Era, such as Jack Egan, Tommy Dorsey's great publicist during most of that band's tenure.

However, what made the attitude of the jazz-sheet writers toward "sweet bands" look ridiculous is epitomized by Simon's obvious adoration of Glenn Miller. That band could hardly be listed in the same category with Duke Ellington, Woody Herman or Tommy Dorsey on up-tempo material. The piece that drew initial attention to Glenn was his arrangement of "Sunrise Serenade," recorded on Decca. The band was and is known among its legions of fans for its sweet style rather than the few "swinging" RCA-Victor sides, such as "Tuxedo Junction."

Miller's up-tempo stuff hardly "swung." Its beat was stiff and stodgy, unexciting. Take it from Hal McIntyre, a Miller saxist through most of the band's history and a confidant of Miller. I had dinner with Hal one evening in Washington, D.C., and the conversation inevitably got around to the Miller band and Miller himself. When I mentioned the way the band drew fans and how they congregated around the bandstand instead of dancing, Hal's rejoinder was, "Hell, they gathered around the stand because they couldn't dance too well to our beat. We got a lot of them out on the floor when we went to the sweet stuff, though."

So, I believe that my disagreement with the way the jazz sheet writers climbed all over the sweet bands has merit (one writer once referred to Sammy Kaye's instrument as "sub-gum clarinet").

The band business was not artistic. It was a business. Leaders formed bands to make money. And if a musician with sufficient talent, guts, or financial backing planned a band and was level-headed enough to realize that he lacked the ability to handle a so-called "jazz" group, and therefore went to a sweet style, why should he suffer castigation from sheets that told him he was on the wrong side of the tracks?

As uneducated musically as I was, I soon found that my ear appreciated performances, arrangements (charts) by full ensembles or soloists as well as any writer. And I solidly enjoyed jazz in all forms, particularly Dixieland. Jazz, incidentally, is a much maligned word. The "jazz" sheet writers applied the word to almost anything that wasn't sweet. To differentiate between a Guy Lombardo and a Tommy Dorsey or Duke Ellington they labeled the latter "jazz" combinations.

Ellington's band was closer to "jazz" in its performances than any group in existence during the big band era.

One of the strangest things I found during my run on *Variety*, and I have absolutely no clue as to why, was that I could sit in a place like Meadowbrook or the Cafe Rouge, talking up a storm with friends, yet hear every little thing the band I was reviewing was doing.

After a review I wrote on Charlie Spivak's Orchestra was printed, Charlie called me to say thanks. He said, "But I don't understand how you could write anything about the band. I watched you a good part of the evening while we were on the stand and you were talking all the time."

But, to get back briefly to the sweet bands, they were formed in every case for a specific reason and the arrangements they featured were not usually written to be played by crack musicians. So, the musicianship was not always the best, thus the bands were not the best. Yet they had a place in the overall scheme of the "big band era."

Not every music lover was astute enough musically to appreciate Duke Ellington, Stan Kenton, or Count Basie. For some, the sweet bands provided the music they could enthusiastically enjoy. Considering the legions of music fans Guy Lombardo and Sammy Kaye and all the other sweet bands pleased, there would not have been much of an "Era" without them.

CHAPTER 10

Duke Ellington

The Duke Ellington Orchestra was unquestionably one of the greatest combinations of musicians ever to blow a note. And, as I later determined, it had been around longer than any of its rival bands.

Unfortunately, because it was Black, in its early days it did not get the opportunities afforded bands not nearly as great.

In the spring of 1940, after I'd been writing music news for a short time my boss advised that I had been earmarked to do a record review column. It was then I discovered the Duke. In the initial package of new releases from RCA-Victor was a disk carrying Duke's "Cotton Tail" and "Never No Lament." I flipped. I quickly caught up on Duke's previous releases.

The Ellington Orchestra came within an eyelash of surpassing the Benny Goodman outfit as the most exciting I ever heard. Different in style from the driving Goodman combination, it reached the same point of extreme excitement with subtle, moody arrangements and impeccable performances.

I was in Chicago on business one night in the early 50's having dinner with an agency man, when he mentioned Duke was working a spot on Randolph. I had an 11 p.m. flight reservation back to New York, but I decided I had to listen to Duke for an hour or so. I was so entranced that time slipped by and I kept missing my departure hour, forcing me to make new reservations for later flights. I simply could not tear myself away from that band. In that low-ceilinged room its impact was just tremendous. By the time I left, when the place closed, I was giddy. I reached my Long Island home only in time to take a shower, change clothes, and leave for my New York office.

My wife found it hard to believe my dallying in Chicago was with music provided by a band whose output may never die.

Ellington and his men wrote most of the instrumentals for which the band was known almost the world over. And the titles they applied were both sex-oriented and amusing. "Flaming Sword" and the later "Warm Valley" were among the best they devised. The connotation of those titles caused half of Harlem to fall out of bed with glee when a disk jockey announced them or when the band performed either on a late-night broadcast.

Both arrangements were great, but they were nowhere near the Duke's "Mood Indigo," "Sophisticated Lady," "I Let a Song Go Out of My Heart," "Never no Lament," "Satin Doll," "In My Solitude," "Cotton Tail" and many others.

I haven't counted, but I believe the Duke Ellington Orchestra originated more long-lasting hits than almost any other standout band of "The Era", including Miller, the Dorseys, James. But, not Benny Goodman's.

There was one other unusual comparison between Benny's band and Duke's. Benny included black musicians among his men, while the Duke had a white musician (drummer Louis Bellson) for a number of years. Bellson was married to one of the finest black female performers, Pearl Bailey.

It was a sad day when that band folded.

CHAPTER 11

Glenn Miller

Glenn Miller was a "studio" musician in the early days of radio, along with most of the other bandleaders, great instrumentalists of the time. But, whereas the Benny Goodman, Harry James, Tommy Dorsey, and other great bands were more or less formed around their leader's soloist talent, Miller rarely played solo trombone.

The Glenn Miller Orchestra's huge success in the late 30's and early 40's after a brief struggle and the reverence with which its fans still regard that band, more then fifty years after its leader's untimely death, is to me amazing.

The band never did anything for me. Never once did I get even a modicum of excitement from its performance. I thought its music was pretty, precise, and completely blah, which is about as far out as you can get in being contrary to public opinion.

I reviewed Miller's early recordings—"Sunrise Serenade" (Decca), then "In The Mood," "Tuxedo Junction," and the others on Bluebird that kicked off the band like a skyrocket. I gave them good notices mainly because, as I recall, the arrangements were different rather than exciting. The only recording of his that I really appreciated was "String of Pearls," an outstanding side.

But I never believed Miller could take the country by storm, as he did, in view of the exciting bands then in existence, such as Duke Ellington, Benny Goodman, and Tommy Dorsey. They played rings around Miller on up-tempo arrangements.

Miller's clarinet-lead style unquestionably was the most attractive big band sound ever devised. I questioned hundreds of young people all over the country during occasional road trips with the Ralph Flanagan Orchestra, which admittedly was patterned after Miller's style and was the No. 1 band of the early 50's, and I found that Miller's tremendous popularity was due more to his "sweet" style than the up-tempo material, some of which was great but most of which was stiff.

Yet, as I have said, Miller caught public fancy like no other; additionally his fans got deeper into their idol than the followers of other great bands. They proved absolutely fanatic and the deeper-dyed still are.

One such I watched closely over a period of time was my ex-partner, Herb Hendler, who spent a good part of his early life as an executive with RCA-Victor, which recorded and marketed Miller's discs. Hendler twice pocketed handsome amounts by aping Miller. The first time was when he (after leaving RCA) formed Rainbow Records with a money-man I accidentally set him up with and who financed the making of an album titled "A Tribute to Glenn Miller." Unfortunately, Hendler had the balls to put a shot of Miller in his Air Force uniform on the cover. It began doing very well in the record marts until the Miller estate got wind of it and put a fly in the ointment, serving a cease-and-desist order plus demanding an accounting of earnings.

The second time occurred when Hendler returned to RCA after the war as a promotion man and induced the company's execs to promote a new Miller band. For this very successful project he brought in Perry Como's music arranger, Ralph Flanagan, who he knew could copy Miller very closely, since he had done the Rainbow album. And the stodgy Flanagan would follow his directions implicitly.

But, to get back to Miller himself. He was a cold, calculating man very difficult to talk with, arrogant about the success of his band, dictatorial and utterly lacking in common courtesy. But, those traits did not and do not have anything to do with my reaction to his orchestra.

I clearly recall the first time I heard the band and ran into Mr. Miller, whom I had not ever met. I'd been assigned to "cover" the band at the Glen Island Casino, New Rochelle, New York. Miller was making a tremendous impact on the industry and his remote broadcasts from the Casino were gathering legions of fans.

As a *Variety* staff reporter and reviewer I carried a fair amount of weight. Local booking agents and ballroom operators all over the country, potential buyers all, were subscribers. So, when I attended an "opening" the bandleader and/or his manager made it a point to stop by my table and make conversation over a drink. The routine was then and is to this day simple, everyday courtesy to the media.

I didn't seek special attention from performers, because (1) I didn't take my position seriously, though I was intent about it, and (2) stars of any magnitude never impressed me; I wouldn't walk around the corner to meet one (which irritated a few I might name), and (3) I never worried about the check on assignment. If the house didn't pick it up, which happened more often than not, *Variety* was well-heeled.

At any rate when I showed up at Glen Island, George Evans, Miller's press agent and a very able man whom I knew well, mentioned to Miller that I was in the "house."

Miller asked (Evans later told me), "Does he want to see me?"

George answered, "I don't know."

"Well," said Miller, "if he does, let him ask."

I laughed when Evans relayed the conversation. As I said, I didn't then know Miller at all, had at that point written very little about his band. Consequently, his reaction to me seemed plain stupid and somewhat mystifying.

With his stiff-necked attitude toward someone who just might help him even slightly, Miller revealed himself to me as a first-rate putz who wasn't smart enough to butter his own bread, in contrast to Tommy Dorsey, who had brains enough for a half-dozen like Miller. As time went on Miller never improved his position.

From then on our relations went steadily downhill. I never knew why and never bothered to find out. But, my response to his behavior couldn't help but be harmful to Miller's *Variety* print-out. Like any newspaperman with friends, punches are occasionally pulled. I was no different.

Miller took a dim view of almost anything I wrote thereafter—good, bad, or indifferent. I had a number of disputes with him directly or through the people surrounding him, with the exception of his manager Don Haynes, an immensely likable and capable man with whom I was on a very friendly basis. Strangely enough, Mrs. Haynes, who worked in Miller's New York office, reflected Miller's attitude.

Miller was often petty. One of the *Variety* stories to which he objected violently was a dilly, in view of his #1 rating. It makes my point about him: The band had been booked for weeks into the Sunnybrook Ballroom in Pottstown, Pennsylvania. Owner Ray Hartenstine, seeking the best possible turnout of fans—for his financial sake as well as Miller's—ranged wider than usual in promoting the date, doing disk jockey shows, seeing newspapermen, setting out window cards, etc. Naturally, he handed out more than the usual number of passes.

The date was a resounding success. Perhaps Hartenstine, who was a heavy drinker, somehow annoyed Miller. At any rate, when manager Haynes collected the band's share of a beaucoup box office take he showed Miller the report which, of course, detailed the extra large number of promotional passes.

Miller hit the ceiling. Even though his take was in fancy figures and very likely that way because of Hartenstine's efforts, Miller implied the promoter was trying to steal a few dollars. He demanded the figures be reworked and the extra passes be deleted. For a relative pittance, Miller humiliated one of the most honest ballroom operators in the country. His action was pure chicken-shit.

I got wind of the story because Howard Sinnott, GAC's one-night booker, was aghast at the stupidity of Miller's action. He told me. I checked with Hartenstine, who reluctantly verified that it happened. I printed the story, but it was not given much prominence, which proved no one was out to cut Miller a new ass.

The leader went off like an A-bomb. He'd had enough of *Variety's* darts, he ranted. He sent Evans to see my boss, Abel Green, and demanded that *Variety*, meaning me, get off Miller's back and begin treating the #1 band in the country as it should be treated.

"Like royalty?" Abel asked.

Evans, a great con man and excellent promotion rep, shot back, "Sure, why not?"

That wasn't the only time I clashed with Miller over his conviction that no one should tarnish his image. In a conversation one night with an MCA executive I came across the information that Guy Lombardo's "average check" at the Roosevelt Grill was over $6.00 per person. It was an intriguing statistic, often discussed among people such as Frank Dailey, owner and operator of the then nationally known Meadowbrook. However, by itself it meant nothing.

I set out to do a survey—a money story, the lifeblood of *Variety's* existence. I vaguely was aware of what some of the other more pop-style bands were racking up on location and knew the figures weren't close to those claimed for Lombardo.

I checked every big band hotel spot across the country by phone and in person and wrote a most interesting story. Lombardo's average clearly proved him top-dog at luring the monied crowd. Jimmy Dorsey, a smash hit at that point because of his Decca Record hits, but running #3 and #4 in most polls, ran second with just under $4.00 per person average. Tommy Dorsey, then at the Cafe Rouge, New York, came third with an average of $2.40. Miller's average at Glen Island and Meadowbrook was $1.60 and $1.80, respectively.

There were others, of course, but the above were the topmost.

The story got a great reaction. It more or less proved that the longer a band had been prominent the more it retained a hard core of fans, who eventually became financially able to follow a band anywhere.

Being the newest kid on the block, catering to young fans— the "Coca-Cola" set—Miller was low man on this totem pole. His fans were too young to spend important money.

Talk about Mt. Helena. Miller blew high and wide. He swore the story was designed specifically to make him look bad. He called me and was further infuriated when I told him, "I don't make the figures, I only report them. If you had any sense you'd realize that story could not possibly have been meant to harm you. I draw a salary to report what's interesting to the trade. That's *Variety's* and my purpose and no one, least of all you, will tell me what I can and cannot write. You were included as a statistic only because you are today the strongest draw among the new bands."

Miller wasn't satisfied. Again he sent Evans to go head-to-head with Abel Green and again Evans came out with a bruised forehead.

Miller's pettiness was not confined to his press clippings. Early in 1951 I met in Washington, D.C., with Hal McIntyre, who had played sax with Miller and was Miller's closest confidant. He was now leading his own band, partly financed by Miller. Over dinner, we somehow got on the subject of Glenn, although my main interest was in talking about managing Hal's new band, with Hendler.

Hal told me how, in order to maintain discipline in the Miller band, he and Glenn would select the next musician to be fired. The selectee need not have done anything to draw Miller's ire. It was simply a means of keeping his men in fear.

In those days a Miller sideman drew perhaps three times the annual salary of a musician with Tommy Dorsey, for example, simply because the Miller band was doing so many lucrative things, such as the five-time-a-week Chesterfield radio show. Losing his job was a blow to the musician jettisoned. But the others remembered.

Miller's death was somewhat unnecessary. As is well-known, he disappeared during World War II in an aircraft flying from

England to France. Perhaps what is not as well known is that Miller and his Air Force pilot had been out all night trying to drink the local pubs dry. Not scheduled to take off for Paris until later in the morning, the pair showed up at the airfield at dawn and insisted their plane be readied for flight. The pilot had to pull rank to get his way. They were warned of bad weather conditions over the Channel, but disregarded all warnings and took off.

Don Haynes, Miller's manager, who joined the service with Glenn told me the whole story when I was his guest at the Joe Louis/Billy Conn fight at Yankee Stadium in 1949.

Haynes had followed Miller three days later with the full orchestra. When they landed at Paris, Miller did not meet the band. No one in Paris Air Force circles had seen Miller or his pilot and were not aware they had left England. Neither had checked in.

They later were classed as missing and presumed lost.

To this day not a shred of evidence has surfaced to support any guess as to what happened.

It isn't generally known is that Miller had a very strong premonition before going overseas that he would not come back. Just prior to going into service, Miller's band was playing a date in Boston. He phoned Cork O'Keefe, a close friend of mine, one of the original partners with Tom Rockwell in the General Artists Corporation, manager of the famed Casa Loma Orchestra, and a Hall-of-Famer of the Big Band industry.

Miller asked O'Keefe if he would fly to Boston to meet with him. Cork did so.

Miller explained: "Cork, you know I'm going into the Air Force to lead a band. In a few weeks I'm going overseas. I've got a strong feeling I'm not coming back and I hope you'll do me a favor."

Miller asked O'Keefe to assume the personal management contracts he (Glenn) held with Tex Beneke, Ray Eberle, The Modernaires, Marion Hutton, and others.

Miller wanted Cork in the picture because he knew O'Keefe was as honest as a man can be, that if Miller did return from service O'Keefe immediately would return to him the contracts he outlined. Meanwhile, Miller's people would receive excellent management and advice from Cork. The latter, in return, would be repaid by participating in the earnings of the contractees.

Miller also said that if he did return from service, he planned to organize his own booking agency and management firm and he would like O'Keefe to join the venture.

Cork was one of the most respected and admired people in the band business and it would have been a tremendous feather in Miller's cap to corral him for such an effort.

O'Keefe rejected Miller's proposals. He was then devoting all his time to the still very active Casa Loma band, plus music publishing interests. He did not want added responsibilities and did not need additional income.

The conversation remained poignant to O'Keefe more than 40 years later. He told me about it as we returned from church services in New York for our close friend Connie Boswell of the original Boswell Sisters, the forerunner of such acts as the Andrews Sisters and the McGuire Sisters.

CHAPTER 12

Harry James

Virtually all successful performers had a "hook." Al Jolson's was his black-face one-knee approach to "Mammy." Jack Benny had his fiddle. Later, on radio and in TV it was his consummate timing, developed over years in "vaudeville."

For the big band leaders who were outstanding instrumentalists, their instruments were the hook by which they were instantly recognizable.

Harry James had two hooks—one, he played extremely well, and the other he acquired when he married Betty Grable.

When James wed Grable he provided himself with a hook that made him a lot of money. It also made him on occasion a very nasty man.

Harry was never the most likable personality in the big band business; his exciting trumpet did not necessarily make him a bandleader or his organization a great band. He was "one of the boys"—a musician who reached powerful name value in the eyes of band followers through a half-dozen or so Columbia recordings with a studio band.

James was a great musician but he didn't have many "smarts." During the war, his band played Frank Dailey's Terrace Room in Newark, New Jersey. After the job, he, a couple of music publishers, Dailey, and I were sitting around having a nightcap. Suddenly, James jumped up.

"Gotta go, fellas, I've got 21 notches in the dresser already this week and I want to cut a few more."

On the way back to the Coast he and Betty Grable stopped in Reno and were married.

Later, whenever James and his band were scheduled to set out on a cross-country tour of one-nighters, which was where the big money was, the agents in the various MCA offices (New York, Chicago, Dallas) went to work. They never said so outright, but they managed to hint to promoters buying James that "Betty will be along."

The ballroom owners let drop here and there in their dealings with local newspapermen and radio disk jockeys that they thought Grable would be with Harry this time out. (Harry Moss, the New York one-night manager for MCA, was my source. He didn't like tricking his customers.) The ploy never failed. On dance-night promoters would need an army of police to control the traffic fighting its way into the ballroom.

Grable's presence could almost be felt, so strong was the power of suggestion.

But Betty was rarely there. Usually she was keeping the Hollywood home fires burning or on location for a new picture.

However, she did go out with James often enough to make the promise believable.

James amassed a fortune heavy enough to support a horse-racing stable. He knew well the role Betty unwillingly played and resented it deeply. All anyone had to do to risk a punch in the nose was to repeatedly ask, "Where's Betty?" Harry seemed to take it as an affront to his personality and his band's drawing power if anyone even remotely implied that Betty had anything to do with his band's success. He became so paranoid over "Where's Betty?" that he once spit out of a bus window at fans in a passing car craning necks and asking, "Where's Betty?"

The road bands James led never seemed to match the fire of his own performances, except one combination he worked with in the East late in his career. In my opinion, his bands were sloppy because James himself was basically a sideman rather than a leader. Too, it's likely he spent so much time under Benny Goodman's "Ray" he would not subject his own men to such domination.

But that discipline is what made great bands.

One of James' biggest record hits was "Sleepy Lagoon." Tommy Dorsey had recorded the song for RCA-Victor's Red (Classical) label and it was awaiting release. Tommy felt it would be a sales smash for him. But, probably with the connivance of the publisher Harry recorded it for Columbia's pop label and the company rushed its release. It beat Tommy Dorsey's version to the market and became one of Harry's long-time sellers and one of his biggest live requests. It is a great recording. (U.S Copyright Law empowers the publisher of a new song to control it to some extent by permitting the withholding of a license of a first recording, if the publisher chooses. Once that first license is issued, however, any performer or company can record a song and apply for a license, which cannot be withheld.)

Since Dorsey had recorded his version for RCA-Victor's Classical label, it didn't figure to sell as well as a "pop" version. So it's probable the publisher gave James and Columbia the nod for selfish reasons.

The incident burned Tommy. But he himself was at fault because, as he mentioned to me, he had told James about the song.

The "Lagoon" disk joined James' great hits, "I Don't Want to Walk Without You," "I Cried for You," "I Had the Craziest Dream."

However, it is Harry's cut of "You Made Me Love You" that I remember best—and perhaps so do his fans, but for different reasons.

When I received the record for review my brains took a vacation. Because the arrangement was so schmaltzy and so far from James's usual approach I had a negative reaction without thinking about the performance. The review I wrote wasn't complimentary.

Later, after the recording was a best-seller, I received a tear sheet of the *Variety* record-review page in the mail. Written across it was, "Were you kidding?"

CHAPTER 13

Stan Kenton

I first heard of Stan Kenton when reports of a great new band at a ballroom at Balboa Beach, California, began filtering east. It was so new it hadn't yet achieved a single national radio network wire, then so vitally important to all bands. Therefore I did not hear the band until I was assigned to review its East Coast debut at the Roseland Ballroom, then on Broadway, just off Times Square.

The band knocked me out.

Stan was an intense young leader who knew what he wanted. He had formed an organization that was decidedly different from any then in existence. It was wildly exciting and eventually very successful, even though after a full evening of listening one felt as though he'd taken a physical pounding. The word to describe some of its arrangements: ponderous.

One of the Broadway wags in Lindy's described the band as sounding like "a plane crash at LaGuardia Field." Another cracked, "You don't kick that band off—you count it down."

I liked Stan immediately. He seemed shy, yet was implacable about what he was trying to accomplish. I got a great kick out of talking with him and did so at every opportunity. He seemed to feel the same way. He seemed always to be searching for criticisms or comments about his band and what he was trying to do with it, which he then culled and turned to whatever advantage possible.

I was unique among the relatively small group of writers on the various trade publications devoted to the band business, in that I was not a musician, didn't know the first thing about music, and really did not want to know. My job on *Variety* was to offer what might be termed the "commercial" reaction to anything we might be assigned to review and criticize. That is, how will it do monetarily? Will it draw box office customers? Will it make money?

My only attribute, I eventually discovered, was a good ear. I found that I easily recognized good and bad performances by full bands, soloists, singers, etc. I appreciated all the nuances involved.

One day I happened to be in Cincinnati on business. I ran into Kenton on Vine Street and we repaired to a nearby bar. We sat and talked for almost the entire afternoon while he slowly siphoned from me exactly why I reacted as I did in some of my published comments on the band's performances. I had pointed out that I felt the band's "book" of arrangements was topheavy with heavy-handed writing—that it did not contain enough "light" material to permit listeners a bit of breathing space.

Several months later the band opened at the Commodore Hotel in New York. For Stan's run, in deference to the verve with which the band operated, the bandstand was moved from directly opposite the entrance to the Century Room to the far end of the rectangular room. Had the bandstand remained opposite the hotel lobby entrance (its usual position) there would have been some uncomfortable times for the lobby denizens.

I had no more than gotten seated when Stan bounced off the stand and announced he had something to show me. "Next set I'll play something entirely new," he said. "Let me know what you think of it," as though I was some judge and jury (but that's the kind of guy he was). Then he proceeded to play "The Peanut Vendor." The arrangement is a classic among Kenton fans and it's high among the greatest big band arrangements ever written.

Pete Rugolo, incidentally, did most, if not all of Kenton's arrangements.

One point that highlights the difference between *Variety* and the so-called "jazz" sheets then in existence is contained in a comment made by George Simon of *Metronome* at almost the same time I made a note relative to Stan's style of conducting.

Kenton's Orchestra played a concert at Carnegie Hall, an event of which Stan was immensely proud, rightly so. Simon took Stan over the coals for his "bombastic" conducting style. A tall man, Stan liked to flap his arms, wave only his hands at arms' length, and go into other gyrations when conducting. Simon didn't think much of what was normal for Stan. In an almost coincident issue of *Variety* I commented that "Kenton's arm-flapping style of conducting is in itself a form of showmanship."

Simon was looking at Stan's methods from a strictly musical viewpoint and felt, apparently, that his gyrations reduced the great musical impact of the band. I took the "commercial" viewpoint, feeling that the style of conducting added interest to the overall impact of the band. Later, when Kenton's Orchestra was the basis of a weekly TV broadcast, the director often focused his cameras on Stan's arm-waving.

Performers have looked for a "hook" from time immemorial. Kenton's "hook" was his conducting, although it was minor and he did not intend it as such.

Kenton died an unfortunate early death and, though the "Big Band Era" had long since subsided, the music industry prematurely lost a great musical mind.

CHAPTER 14

Count Basie

I also knew, but not very well,
Count (Bill) Basie. I used to meet him under the strangest conditions, which I didn't ever have explained.

I banked at the Chase Manhattan Radio City branch. On
occasion when I went in to put or take I'd see Bill standing near
the door. Each time he had a check issued by the Willard
Alexander Agency, which handled his bookings.

Whether the agency anticipated he would deposit the check
elsewhere or had other ways of turning it into cash, I have no idea.
Chase officials (squares) didn't know him and would not cash the
check. "Base" would just stand near the door and wait for anyone
he knew. On a number of occasions I okayed it and he got his
money.

I cannot fathom the whole thing to this day. It would have been simple for Alexander to "okay for cash," since the agency must have banked at the same branch. Its offices were across the street.

At any rate, the first I ever heard of the Count Basie Orchestra was from John Hammond, the eminent jazz critic, then attached to Columbia Records. He touted the band to anyone and everyone after hearing it on a visit to Kansas City, Bill's home town. John promised that it would knock me out. It did.

When the Basie band hit New York it opened at the Famous Door, on 52d Street, a 40's hangout for the music biz of that time. The band drew rave reviews and never looked back—to Kansas City, that is.

It was a great combination which I rate well within the Top 10 of the standouts of the Big Band Era.

CHAPTER 15

Frank Sinatra

The teen on the roof of the cab tried hard to drive his foot through the "sky-view" glass. Two others lay prone on the engine hood peering through the windshield. A fourth pounded on a rear door glass, snarling that he was going to break my head. He didn't appreciate my closing the window on his arm, which had been ripping the lapel from my jacket.

The four were part of a howling mob of some 1,000 Chinatown, New York-area kids and a few adults who had me trapped and scared silly. Their numbers grew by the minute as more and more bodies tumbled out of the steaming tenements that lined the lower East Side's Mulberry Street, attracted by the din.

All were pushing to see "the guy in the cab."

The word was he was Frank Sinatra. It wasn't. Frank, at that point, was preparing to high-jump a restaurant's backyard fence

117

and run through to the next street, leaving me and the cabbie to face the "music" of his adoring fans.

The cabbie was as upset as I at the battering we were taking, since he owned the cab. We were being rocked by a bunch of the more playful, so he figured he'd extricate us. He tried low gear. Nothing. The hack didn't move. Reverse. A standstill. Those kids actually held the cab (of course, he could have moved if he'd stepped on it, but he was afraid of hurting someone).

We sat. The cabbie didn't dare shut off the engine. The two kids on the hood had collapsed it and he figured to let well enough alone.

We were sitting ducks.

The mob milled and danced, everyone screaming. In the middle of it, I recall a weird thought: From the tenement roof above we must look like a piece of cake being swarmed over by a sea of ants.

At least forty minutes later I heard an alien sound—the clanging of a bell, then a siren.

"Sit tight," the cabbie yelled, "the cavalry is coming." Sit tight? Hell, I wasn't going anywhere. That's all I'd been doing, meanwhile telling myself that I'd had my fill of Frank's "adoring fans," a misnomer for animals.

The huge Elizabeth Street Precinct emergency truck inched toward us, siren, horn, and bell blasting away, searchlights scanning the mob, squad members clearing its path of darting teens. The huge vehicle slowly moved closer. It was a wild scene that I vividly remember fifty years later.

Even then those kids were not afraid of the cops.

Finally, the huge truck's front bumper nestled against ours. Reversing, it began backing up Mulberry Street while we kept bumpers tight. Now the squad kept the rear clear. Slowly we backed, locked together.

The two vehicles crossed Canal Street while the police held rush-hour traffic. At a signal, the cab slowed and the truck kept moving. When we got room, we shot around and took off like a scared rabbit, yelling our thanks. Meanwhile, we'd been told to meet Frank at Canal and West Streets.

We drew to a stop. A grinning Sinatra dropped into the seat beside me. The first words out of his mouth were not, "Are you guys OK?". His first words were, "Now you know what it has been like for me these last months."

After a few choice words about his fans, we laughed, but it was strained. We were all shook up. Those lower East Side kids were a tough mob. They handled like rag dolls the cops initially sent to get us out of the restaurant in response to the owner's call for help.

On that evening, a Friday, I had returned to *Variety* headquarters after a day of chasing news to find a message from Frank asking that I call a backstage phone in a CBS Radio broadcast studio almost around the corner. When I reached him, Frank asked whether I would come by, he had something to show me (he was substituting for an ill Perry Como on the latter's nightly fifteen minute broadcast).

When I joined him, Frank showed me the layout of an ad he contemplated placing in the next issue of *Variety*. He wanted my opinion of its content before giving the okay to place it to George Evans, his and one of Broadway's standout press agents.

When we finished, Frank suggested I stay for the broadcast and go to dinner with him and Manie Sachs, a Vice President of CBS and President of its Columbia Records subsidiary. They were being entertained by a music publisher friend and were going downtown to a popular Italian eatery.

I tried to beg off. "I've got to review the new Paramount show," I told Frank. "If I don't get it tonight, I'll have to come in over the weekend." (The New York Paramount then was the country's premier big band/first-run film house. New shows opened on Wednesdays, but I always let a show "settle" before reviewing.)

"Oh, come on," Frank came back. "We'll get you back uptown before the last performance."

Finally I agreed. The people involved were among my best news sources, particularly Manie, with whom I was very close.

When the broadcast was over, the publisher and his wife were on hand. We had to pick up Manie. In those days, limos and entourages were in Sinatra's ever-brightening future. When he was in New York he had a favorite hackie who apparently owned his own cab. Frank paid him by the week, I believe.

When we left the studio, a group of youngsters were waiting. They were a snap to get through, but one chubby youngster, thirteen or fourteen, would not give up. As we turned uptown on Eighth Avenue she was still chasing the cab, running in the middle of the avenue while traffic swirled around her. Suddenly, it opened up and we spurted. I'll never forget the anguish on that round, red face when she realized she didn't have a chance of catching Frank. She epitomized his followers—the gentler variety.

When we reached the restaurant, Frank said, "Let me duck in first." He ran for the door. I thought I saw recognition in the eyes of a youngster standing nearby. I mentioned it as we were seated, and to my dismay, I was correct. In ten minutes there were five kids staring through the huge plate-glass window of the old-fashioned store front. Then there were ten. Then twenty. Then fifty.

All of a sudden there were five hundred screaming fans pressing against the glass and their numbers were growing fast.

Everyone became apprehensive, especially those diners sitting near the window.

We finally realized dinner was over before it began. Frank's presence was ruining appetites and endangering more than a few. Frank himself asked the owner to send for a couple of cops. When they showed they suggested we all go out through the back. Frank said "No, let Bernie and Manie get in the cab while you two hold the crowd back. I don't want them hurt." The mob by then was well over a thousand, the cops told us.

Manie and I approached the front door. Manie said, "You First". He opened the door while the cops held the crowd. I stepped out and started to run across the sidewalk. All hell erupted. Those kids literally passed those cops to the rear. They closed on me. In seconds I lost all my jacket buttons and my bow tie, and had to yank one of my loafers away from a "fan."

I fought my way into the cab, thinking Manie was right behind me. But he'd retreated fast when he saw what happened to me. Before I could force the door closed, a teen began tearing the lapel from my jacket.

It had never occurred to any of us that the kids might take me for Frank on that dimly lit sidewalk. I was shorter than he, but skinny (123 pounds), also had a bow tie, and wore my hair in a similar fashion. Frankly, I don't believe many of the kids in that mob even knew what was going on. It was a hot, muggy night on the Lower East Side and very likely they would have jumped at anything to break the monotony. Frank's name was a catalyst and the cabbie and I felt the brunt of the explosion. I get uneasy even now at the recollection.

Frank and Manie? They went over a backyard divider like a pair of gazelles and were met on the next block and driven to our later rendezvous. The publisher and his spouse stayed for dinner.

Frank's cab dropped me off at the executive entrance to the Paramount. One look and manager Bob Weitman and assistant Bob Shapiro had me pegged for a funeral mass at St. Patrick's Cathedral until I related what had me looking like death warmed over. They couldn't stop laughing. They knew Sinatra fans.

That was not really the first time I'd gotten a first-hand look at Sinatra's wild followers. I was with him one night at a Lucky Strike Hit Parade radio broadcast when he almost lost his life upon exiting the theater. A mob closed in on him and he disappeared. When he came up he was blue in the face. Someone had tried to pull off his bow tie, which wouldn't give. That's when then wife Nancy devised those flimsy bows he later featured.

I must have written something at one later point that annoyed Frank or his press agent, George Evans. I came back to the office one afternoon and found a mob of kids milling around outside. I pushed through and when I reached my desk, Abel Green called down from his dais desk and asked me how I got into the building.

"I walked through those kids," I answered. "Why do you ask?"

"They're looking for you," was his shocking answer. "Can't you hear what they're saying?" Bending a close ear, I got the drift.

No one identified me when I left the office for dinner and at least half the mob was still outside. I simply walked through them again.

I met Frank initially when he joined Tommy Dorsey's Orchestra, "direct from Harry James," then at the Rustic Cabin, Englewood Cliffs, New Jersey, one of the half-dozen or so Big Band bookings in Northern New Jersey. It was built of logs, exactly as its name implied and it could burn easily, which is what eventually happened.

I was with Tommy, sipping coffee in the outer office of his Radio City digs. He was telling me about Sinatra when the door literally banged open and in strutted Frank shouting, "Hi, Harve," Dorsey's name fetish. And I mean strutted.

Frank was good, but not the singer he became after working with Tommy Dorsey for a few years. It has frequently been said that his breath control, which supports his style, evolved as a result of proximity to Tommy's trombone. Breath control is tremendously important to any singer, but particularly to Frank. It is also important to a wind-instrument musician and Tommy was one of the best at his business.

I have heard Frank's singing voice on a number of pre-Dorsey things, particularly his shot on the old Major Bowes Amateur Hour on radio, which he and his group did not win. While the sound was present, the style was only a glimmer. Perhaps it eventually would have shone through without Tommy Dorsey, but it's my opinion that the sexy glissing, which turned all in panties into panting putty, occurred mainly as a result of proximity to Tommy's horn.

Be that as it may, Frank's successes with Tommy and the Pied Pipers were tremendous. Not too long after the smash hit records of "I'll Never Smile Again" and "This Love of Mine," the entourage was booked into the Paramount Theater in New York and I was assigned to review.

Frank's work exhibited such poise and show business savvy and such control over his already wild audience that I was moved to include a line that he was ready to spread his own wings. He finally parted with Tommy in the spring of 1941.

Amazingly, his first solo recording in his own name, a really great cut of Cole Porter's "I've Got You Under My Skin," hit the stands and lay there like yesterday's newspaper.

That strange paradox continued for a couple of years. On records, Frank simply couldn't get himself "locked up" as they say in Brooklyn. His initial hit as a soloist didn't happen until he switched to Columbia with Manie Sachs. It was titled, "Oh What It Seemed to Be," a tune supplied by Tommy Valando, General Professional Manager of Santly-Joy Music Company, who had offered first refusal to Perry Como, then his bosom buddy. Perry rejected the song.

The cut sold over 400,000 copies, a big number at that time, but a pittance for a hit today.

Frank then moved to Capitol Records and again smashed through with a song titled "Young At Heart," also published, by Tommy Valando, who at this point had established his own music publishing business, backed financially by Perry Como.

Frank's fortunes in recording took off then, and he couldn't do much wrong. He got so strong he established his own recording label, Reprise Records. It did so well he sold it to Warner Bros. Communications for a bundle of money.

Sinatra's initial engagement as a soloist was at the Riobamba, New York, a rooftop spot on East 57th Street, supposedly backed by the mob. It didn't last long, but to this day it is frequently noted in print as the site where Frank's solo history was launched.

I was assigned to review. Aside from the fact that he was understandably nervous, Frank's performance was a great job. I stayed for the second show and the difference between the two was like night and day, so quickly did he acclimate himself. He was a star in every sense of the word.

As he grew in stature he appeared in the best spots in the country. The production, presentation and promotion of Frank's personality and his act became, to me, one of the sharpest operations I've ever observed. His bookings were handled by MCA and undoubtedly their brightest brains were bent in his behalf.

The first time he worked the Empire Room of the Waldorf-Astoria Hotel, New York, was an example. About an hour before show time the rheostat controlling the power to the huge chandeliers was reduced slightly. In fifteen minutes another slight cut. Another and then another. Most patrons, busy talking, were only dimly conscious of what was happening. But, as the lights went down the tension went up minute by minute until everyone was wound tight, anticipating. About ten minutes before the show, which was deliberately delayed, waiters fanned out advising all to order up, there would be no service while Frank was on.

By the time Sinatra tripped on with a cup of coffee, singing Redd Evans' "Coffee Song" as an opener, he need only have done a handstand and they would have blown off the roof.

Over the years I've reviewed and criticized some of the greatest musical performers show business has produced. But I have never seen anything to match Frank's performance the night he closed the Riviera in Fort Lee, New Jersey (an undercover gambling spot), which was to be torn down the next day to make room for the Palisades Parkway. I was in management by then and attended with a client and some friends. Frank stepped on that stage to thunderous applause and that was the last alien sound, aside from his voice, that was heard for more than an hour. He went from one familiar standard to another without a word while the crack group of musicians behind him fell smoothly into his leads. One could hear the proverbial pin drop. His listeners were mesmerized by his cockiness, his talent. Anyone who coughed was glared at. The air was electric.

After nearly ninety nonstop minutes, Frank suddenly said "Good Evening, Ladies and Gentlemen." They were his first non-musical words. They were like fire to an explosive charge. The roof rang for minutes on end.

It was a performance I will never forget. It was one of the greatest I've ever witnessed by a talent that will go down in show business history as one of a kind.

In March of 1993 we witnessed an aging Sinatra enthralling TV audiences in tandem with Sammy Davis and Liza Minnelli.

His voice was edging the way of all aging flesh but it was impossible to disagree with anything he did. Everything was there—the talent, timing, and his unique appreciation for great lyrics. But something new was added—mugging.

The performance of those three titans made a "music" lover realize what a terrible fall singing, song writing, and pop music generally have taken since rock took helm.

CHAPTER 16

Perry Como

Most of the great solo singers of the years during and following the Big Band Era succeeded due to the impetus given their careers by Big Band associations. Frank Sinatra is a standout example.

However, on the other side of the ledger there are many examples of stars who hit the jackpot without the push of a nationally known Big Band. Perry Como sang with the little-known Ted Weems orchestra on a Sunday radio show sponsored by a cosmetic house that called itself Varedy of Vienna. He sounded like an imitation Bing Crosby.

I'd never heard of Perry until I was assigned to review his debut as a "house singer" on CBS radio, at $100 a week on a sustaining program (no sponsors). That arrangement was one of the smartest moves ever made by Perry's mentor Tom Rockwell, head of GAC.

Como was under a new contract at NBC at the time (RCA-Victor records plus the parent radio network). However, NBC did not have a spot on the net for Perry and was not contemplating one. Rockwell convinced NBC execs to let rival CBS use Perry on the theory that the exposure would in the end benefit NBC.

Perry remained with CBS through years of radio, then commercial television. When he finally did go back to NBC for a full hour of TV weekly, he was a huge star.

In my first review, I noted that Perry seemed a bit nervous—understandable under the circumstances. Otherwise, the commentary was favorable.

The day after it was printed I received a call from a man named Tommy Valando, whom I didn't know then. He was General Professional Manager of Santly-Joy Music Co., one of the top catalogs among the old-line publishing houses.

Valando climbed all over me for the mildly negative aspects of my criticism of Como. He intimated that I was motivated by my friendship with Billy Burton, Jimmy Dorsey's manager, whose band featured Bob Eberly. Jimmy's band was a stickout due to a string of hit recordings with Eberly vocals.

Apparently Valando and Como looked upon Eberly as a possible rival.

As I said I had never heard of Como before I was assigned to review him. Since I didn't know Valando either, his apparent knowledge of my movements and friends bugged me.

We got into it rather heavily. Suddenly, Valando halted his diatribe and asked if I'd ever met Como, then asked whether I would meet with him. I agreed. That evening I went over to Valando's office in the Brill Building, New York, and found Como to be a very quiet, affable character exactly opposite of what I expected in view of the aggressive way Valando came on in his behalf.

I don't know whether Valando's leap at me was his own idea or prompted by Como. I know that over the years Perry has acquired his "Mr. Nice Guy" tag by having other people do his dirty work. That's not a criticism. To me, it's highly acceptable. I know that when I blow I'm the one who gets in trouble.

I've watched Perry for too many years not to know that my evaluation is correct. The object of any of his negative affection never hears it from him personally. The shaft is always wielded by another.

However, as many times as we've golfed together, been at parties and at each other's homes together, I have always felt a slight reservation in Perry's behavior toward me. I would bet anything that it stems from that initial contact. Como never forgets.

That first meeting between Valando, Como and me began a long friendship that widened into a circle including Dee Belline, Como's brother-in-law; George Paxton, arranger-bandleader; and Mitch Ayres, former bandleader and later musical conductor of Perry's TV programs and RCA-Victor recordings.

We had some wild times together. Perry is a great guy to socialize with. Away from show business he shows little conception of his importance and never forgets old friends, at least the ones he wants to remember.

Perry, Tommy, Paxton and I were all golfers and in the years before either of us made any real money we played together, at a Bayside, Long Island course fairly close to all our homes. Babe Ruth frequented that course when he was a New York Yankee.

Perry is a slow, deliberate golfer. I've always made the funny that you could see him relaxing every muscle, starting with his ears, when he was addressing a shot. By the time he hit it you wanted to scream. Consequently, if there was any traffic behind our foursome it usually began to pile up. (Later, when we were members at

Paumonak and Garden City Country Clubs, members who saw Perry in the locker or dining rooms would rush to tee off first.)

Once at Bayside we teed off early. No one was in sight. About the seventh or eighth hole I noticed a twosome moving up on us. By the twelfth hole they were pressing. On the short fourteenth we were putting out when a ball landed on the green among us. Paxton and I blew instantly and in seconds were in a shouting match. We were advised to move or the guy who hit the ball would come down and help us. Paxton advised him if he did he'd better bring a club because he'd need it.

We heard a mutter. I turned around and saw Como walking toward the next tee with his hand over his mouth mumbling, "Two thousand worth of new crockery and these bastards want to start a fight." And he was the cause of the whole thing.

On New Year's Eve, 1947, Valando and his wife hosted a house party. It was the year of the big day-after-Christmas snowstorm. Long Island was inundated. Few cars were moving. But the Long Island Railroad, which had a reputation for halting service if anyone spit on the tracks, was operating.

Valando hired a horse and sleigh. Tommy, Pax, and I lived fairly close so the sleigh had an easy time picking up George and Mary and Lorraine and me. Perry came in from Manhasset on the railroad and Dick Voltter (General Professional Manager of Shapiro-Bernstein, one of the largest old publishers) came out from the city. The sleigh got them. Dee and Mitch couldn't make it. Their garages were buried and streets not yet open, almost a week after the storm.

We had a ball. Tommy rented a late Hollywood film and we leisurely got loaded and overstuffed awaiting the New Year. Soon after midnight Tommy glanced out the window and saw the sleigh, the horse blanketed to the ears. Nearby lived Charlie Trotta, another pal, manager of Rosemary Clooney and Tony Pastor's orchestra. He'd been invited but couldn't make it. One of his youngsters was very ill.

Tommy decided we should make a New Year's call. We piled into the sleigh, which, I can imagine, didn't make the horse too happy. Pulling that load through the snow-filled, unplowed streets of Murray Hill, Flushing, Long Island, was not a lark.

Trotta filled in our empty spaces with more booze. On the way home we got frisky, yelling like Comanches, urging the horse on. The cold didn't bother us one bit.

A good rider, Pax climbed out on the shafts. I was loaded enough that I followed. The horse was laboring and the two jerks on his back didn't make it easier. Then he'd had enough. Between jumps he bucked and George and I sailed off in one piece, luckily to one side. Locked together, we somersaulted and landed in a snowbank, me underneath. We lay there. Then we heard Perry yelling, "Where's Bernie?" He could see only Pax. I was having a hell of a time breathing because I was head down. George whispered, "Keep quiet," and stood up. Como and the others were running around like madmen trying to find me. Perry thought I was under the horse. They began to get real upset, so I stood up. I should have stayed down. For scaring them I got dumped on.

Perry bought a house in Flower Hill, Long Island, along the sixth hole of the North Hempstead Golf Club. He sought to join, since it was literally in his backyard. At that time Perry Como wasn't yet a household word. The membership committee rejected him. Show-business people were verboten.

Years later, when Perry was a huge star they made overtures. Perry told them what they could do with their acreage.

Which brings to mind an experience I had before being accepted at the Garden City Country Club. Originally, we all were

members at Paumonak, a tough championship course that for
some reason I could beat, enjoying there a PGA-rated nine handicap. It was hilly, long, and tough. It was sold for a housing development and we had to get out. It was arranged for at least 60 members to move to the Garden City club.

I did not know Garden City was restricted. P.C., Valando, Dee,
Sammy Kaye and all the guys were automatically accepted. Mitch
was, too, though he was Jewish and running under the Christian
Science banner. (It wasn't a dodge; his young daughter once
became deathly ill and almost died because he and Georgia
refused medical aid. Fortunately, they reneged in time and the
daughter recovered.)

I was not immediately accepted. I was invited to the office of
the Chairman of the Membership Committee to be interviewed. I
was annoyed, but I went.

During the questioning it dawned on me that, because of my
first name, he thought I was Jewish. I listened to this guy until I'd
had enough. I finally exploded and told the s.o.b. to stick the
G.C.C.C. up his ass, that I'd been born a Roman Catholic, attended all parochial schools, knew as many priests as he did; that my
father was a Fourth-Degree plus a Grand Knight of the Knights of
Columbus as well as president of the Holy Name Society in our
home parish, which I never went near, I added, because of ass-
holes like him.

I stalked out after asking him if he knew so much Catholicism
how come he never heard of St. Bernard, for whom my Irish-
Scotch-German parents named me. I was livid.

The guy started a campaign of calling me, at home and at my
office. I wouldn't talk with him. Finally, I quieted down. All my
friends were members and if I wanted to play and enjoy their com-

pany I had to back off. I became a member, but it stuck in my craw for years.

Perry bought the Flower Hill, Long Island, house late in 1945 or thereabouts. In May 1946 I acquired one of the first Chryslers off the post-war production line ($1,745). Frank Dailey, of Meadowbrook, got it for me through a dealer friend. The following Saturday it was arranged that I'd pick up Perry for golf. As we were sitting in his kitchen bay window having coffee, he happened to see the car.

I was still on *Variety*. Since it is known newspaper minions do not often become millionaires, Perry asked who owned the new car. When I said I did, he flipped.

"How the hell can you buy a new car?" he asked. "I can't, I've got to roll that old heap of mine [pre-war Packard] for a while yet." This from a guy who a few years later didn't want to take out of RCA-Victor a million or so in accumulated record royalties because he disliked paying the heavy tax burden. RCA was between a shit and a sweat because the IRS then demanded heavy taxes on undistributed royalties.

On a beautiful May morning Perry, Pax, Tommy, and I were down for an early teeoff at Paumonak. I was having a late coffee and ran out at the last minute and drove off. Walking down the fairway, I recognized Perry's caddie as Frankie Simon, an old school chum from College Point, Long Island. I'd hit a good drive, but slightly left. The others went slightly right. We parted.

When I was out of hearing Perry apparently remarked, "Look where Bern hit that ball." (I was a long hitter for my size and weight.) Simon piped up: "If you think he hits a golf ball, you should see him hit a cue ball." Perry questioned him and heard for the first time that I played billiards well enough to have given exhibitions against world-championship contenders, a few of whom I'd beaten.

Perry didn't forget. The following August or September, on the occasion of the birthday of his wife, Roselle, Perry gave a dinner party. During its course, Dee and Perry began making remarks about pool sharks. I paid no attention since I didn't know about Simon's revelations.

Finally, Dee said to me, "I understand you're a good man with a cue."

"Where did you get that idea?" I shot back.

"From that caddie friend of yours at Paumonak," Perry offered.

Dee followed with, "Perry just bought a pool table. How about you and me getting into it later?"

I didn't know P.C. had a table and I really had no interest in getting mixed up with either of them since I hadn't played in years. As in any sport, when you lay off billiards for any length of time your "stroke" suffers. It's like losing the timing of hitting a baseball or golf ball. An eye is essential, of course, but the stroke is the meat.

When we reached Como's house, things turned out as I suspected. I was to play Perry. He had been doing a great deal of practicing and, since he was a good athlete, had become a reasonably good player, which I saw immediately. Paxton, Dick Voltter, Al Gallico and Dee began laying it down. Before we started there was $500 or more on the line, most of it on Perry (song-pluggers knew on which side their bread was buttered).

Perry wanted to play a 25-point game, which can last only a few minutes with good players. The score was 23 to 20 in his favor when he missed and set up a difficult leave. I noticed an arrangement of balls and picked a shot that, if not hit correctly, would spread the few remaining balls and let Perry Como run out. If I pulled it off, however, he would be in a jam.

The shot was perfect and Perry could do nothing. He rammed his cue through the balls on the table and I ran out the five I needed to win the game. He called my safety "nigger pool."

I was surprised because he seldom lost his temper. It was hard to explain to someone beaten on his own table with a cue from the rack by a guy who hadn't played for years, that instinct is difficult to ignore. In billiards, as in many other games, "the idea is to prevent your opponent from scoring if you cannot score."

He wasn't placated.

The incident epitomized the rivalry that existed between me and members of our group, particularly Mitch Ayres. This hulk must have weighed 250 and stood about 6'3. I was 5'6 and never weighed more than 123 pounds. Mitch was never a natural at anything. But he was dedicated. (I once caught him playing a few holes alone early in the morning at Garden City and kidded that that was like drinking alone.) He laughed but kept right at it, eventually working down to an eight or nine handicap.

Things inevitably reached the point where the mere mention of my name to Mitch in relation to sports was like a red flag to a bull. At the Green Valley Country Club outside Philadelphia, where Mitch, Pax, Tommy, and I were invited by Manie Sachs, a most unlikely scratch player, Mitch demanded to play me a $100 Nassau. I beat him on the front side by holing a shot out of a trap so deep I couldn't see the flag. We halved the back side but only with the connivance of his caddie. He had hit his second shot right and almost out of bounds. I had an easy nine-iron pitch. When I was in my swing the caddie screamed in my ear, ostensibly because someone was about to pick up Mitch's ball. It still cost him $200.

We had a loose bowling league. At midnight or later, if enough songpluggers were around, we'd go to the Roxy Alleys. Heavy betting was the order. One night at dinner Mitch became annoyed at the joshing he was taking about me.

"I'll bowl you five games, total pins, for anything you want," he challenged.

"How much you want to lose?" I shot back.

Mitch started out with five straight strikes and won the first game by 96 pins. I started the second game with six straight strikes and kept on going. I beat him by 102 total pins. I could have been disabled that time.

Como and our guys were a great bunch of "coffee housers." Perry's favorite was to wear highly polished golf shoes. In the middle of your swing, he'd twist his upended driver resting on a shoe tip. It emitted a slight squeak, just enough to throw you if you were sensitive. If you got to where it didn't bother you, he wouldn't do it, which was just as annoying.

Normally, very little upset me. But, one day Tommy and Pax found out what did. All they had to do was whisper. I guess my reporter's instinct came alive and I'd strain to hear what was being said and then I'd blow the shot.

One of the unique experiences I had while on *Variety* involved Perry's nightly radio broadcast (before TV). Promotion men for TWA and CBS combined to promote the debut of the Constellation into airline service. They dreamed up the idea of doing a broadcast from one of the new aircraft 25,000 feet over Riverhead, Long Island, where RCA's huge overseas antennas were located.

Jo Stafford was Perry's guest.

We took off from LaGuardia Airport loaded with musicians, technicians, producer and director, press people, and a few others. What an eerie feeling, riding a bouncing aircraft while 18 musicians distributed the length of the plane, blew up a background for Perry and Jo.

I have mentioned that Tommy Valando and Perry were like brothers. Tommy lived a little closer to New York than I and we would take turns driving into the city together. One summer morning in the late 40's I picked him up. He got into the car mumbling about an S.O.B.

"Who, me?" I asked.

"Nah," he answered. "I'm talking about Perry."

Tommy explained that he and his bosses had selected a newly written song to become the firm's "No. 1 Plug," meaning it would get full promotional treatment by the entire staff, which Tommy supervised. It was titled "Oh What It Seemed to Be." Such was the nature of their relationship that Tommy confidently expected Perry to record the tune and feature it on his CBS Television broadcasts.

Perry rejected the song. Tommy was incensed. He didn't do anything then to disturb their friendship but I believe, from watching them both for a long time, Tommy took a page from Perry's book: He never forgot.

Perry's attitude did not deter Tommy from going ahead with the song's promotion. As much from a desire for the strongest possible performance rather than spite, Tommy sent it to Frank Sinatra, whose Columbia recording became his biggest hit in sales numbers to that point in his career. It was most notable because Frank had not done well on records immediately after he went solo.

A few years later Frank made a smash of another Valando song titled "Young at Heart." At that point, Tommy was running his own publishing firm, financed by Como.

Perry steamed. The premise of his nightly CBS broadcasts called for him to perform the hit songs as well as standards (unquenchable past hits). There was every reason to perform "Oh What It Seemed" since it was a smash. He wouldn't touch it.

Tommy steamed—again. He'd been cut deep twice by someone he thought to be his closest friend.

I believe that the eventual split between the two and Tommy's behavior, which caused the split, began to fester at that point. But Valando was smart. He tucked it into the back of his head and waited.

A year or so later, Dick Voltter and I had a dinner date with Tommy. We sat drinking and waiting until Tommy showed. The first words out of his mouth were, "Well, I did it."

"You did what?" we chorused.

"I quit," he said.

Dick and I sat with our mouths open. We were dumbfounded. As close as we both were to Tommy, we hadn't the slightest inkling of what he was planning.

"I'm going into publishing with Perry," he said.

Later, George Joy, the co-owner of Santly-Joy, Tommy's boss, complained that I had a hand in Tommy's leaving. He went to my boss and threatened to halt his *Variety* advertising. Lester Santly, Joy's partner, was a director of the ASCAP, and a source of news, the lifeblood of my activity. He dried up like a prune. So I was hurt.

Perry put up the money and Tommy opened Laurel Music Co. It was successful almost from the ribbon cutting. Tommy cultivated the writing team of (Benny) Benjamin and (George) Weiss and they turned out "A, You're Adorable." Another writing team came up with "Young At Heart." (By then I was managing the Ralph Flanagan Orchestra.)

A few years later, there was a split. I happened on Perry's long-time attorney, Jack Katz, aboard the Twentieth-Century Limited, from Chicago to New York, and he told me the whole story. He outlined the financial operations within the companies that boded ill for Tommy.

Katz's revelations brought to mind the one time I was really angry with Tommy. While I was still on *Variety* and the Valando/Como alliance was in high gear, Tommy called and wanted to see me. His purpose was to offer me a monthly check from the companies. We never got far enough to determine what he expected in exchange. It was a stupid move in view of how close we'd been and I angrily told him so.

In view of later events I always wondered whether Tommy put me down on the books and pocketed the money.

There isn't any question in my mind that a fair number of recording and music publishing executives pocketed extra money every month by writing or causing to have written checks to "cash," which purportedly were going to me or other members of the writing fraternity (*Billboard, Downbeat, Metronome*). I'd had many such offers while I occupied a fairly important spot on *Variety* and I turned them all down. But every once in a while you'd get a "knowing" glance from someone with seemingly "inside" information.

In one case, I found that a booking agency owner had brass enough to make company checks out to my name, which he apparently deposited in his personal account. Better than cheating on taxes.

So, Tommy's bid was not that unusual.

Perry walked away from the alliance without a backward glance. He handed the firms over to Tommy lock, stock and barrel. Didn't even recover his initial investment, his attorney told me. I do not believe Tommy and Perry have exchanged one word since. I do know the depth of Como's disappointment.

The music companies launched thusly grew and grew under Valando's guidance. His acquisition of Broadway musical scores widened, presumably due to the great creativity of the writers he managed to "corral." He eventually challenged the huge Chappell Music combine, which for years had a lock on virtually everything coming off Broadway stages. (Chappell set up individual publishing companies for most of the "old guard"—such as Rodgers & Hammerstein, and Rodgers & Hart—consequently had an inside track.)

The importance of the publishing firms originally financed by Como thus became so strong that Valando sold the group in the mid-seventies to Metromedia for a number reported by the trade papers to be $4.500,000. Plus a contract to manage.

The development of the Valando publishing companies is without question one of the greatest success stories ever to come out of Tin Pan Alley. It rivals and surpasses in many ways the story of Lou Levy, who began by managing the Andrews Sisters into a tremendously valuable group of females, upon whom he built a music publishing empire that he also sold to Metromedia for the same numbers—$4,500,000, according to the trade papers.

There was a great difference between the two men, however. Tommy became a country squire, chauffeured limousine and all. Levy took his money and ran to Europe, where in less than ten years, he was reputed to have gone broke.

The kicker is that when Levy returned from England he went to work for Valando in an executive capacity.

Perry set up his own publishing company and named it Roncom after his oldest son, Ronnie. It was purely a holding company, it appeared, run by brother-in-law Dee, who died a few years ago after a stroke. Mickey Glass, Perry's long-time confidant and aide and a former music man, took over the reins.

For many years, Perry refused to do "personal appearances." Soon after his success on records in the early 40's, he played the New York Strand Theater, which then had a big band policy, and the Copacabana, famed New York nitery. That was it. He shut down live bookings though he could have returned beaucoup commissions to GAC, whose owner, Tom Rockwell, supported Perry and his family in the days they didn't have to eat, as they say on Broadway.

At any rate, almost twenty years ago I began seeing ads in the newspapers pointing up "live" appearances by Perry at theaters-in-the-round in Valley Stream, Long Island, Valley Forge, Pennsylvania, and in the Washington, D.C. area.

Lorraine and I went to one of the Valley Forge performances. When we got into the arena, my *Variety* instincts surfaced. I began sizing the house and doing some arithmetic. At a top of $15.00 and hundreds of additional seats at $12.50 and $10.00, I knew why P.C. had gotten off his ass and away from his Jupiter, Florida, home and his fishing trips with Paxton, who had retired to Vero beach. (He is now deceased.)

I figured that the Theater-In-The-Round, where Como put on a performance that floored me, had to provide him with between $500,000 and $750,000 take-home. It led me to believe that the ol' gaffer was doing better than ever.

I still remember that old Packard vs. my new Chrysler.

CHAPTER 17

Dinah Shore

Some years ago I read a serialized interview with Dinah Shore. It detailed how the Eddie Cantor radio program of years ago launched her fabulous career and how Cantor hired her because one of his comedian's daughters heard one of Dinah's records and convinced her father to put the singer on his show.

The way it really went down was as follows: I was having a late lunch at the Gateway Restaurant in Radio City, New York, a spot Dinah knew well. Frank Cooper, then head of the Radio Department of GAC, joined me. The first thing he said was, "Do you know where I can find a girl singer?—There's a good job open and I have no one to submit."

I told him to finish his lunch and I'd show him the best I knew. We walked a block or so to the Center Music Shop, also in Radio City. It was the style then for music stores to have individual booths in which record buyers could listen to product before buying. (We're talking here about 78rpm, two-sided disks, the only thing then available.)

I asked a clerk for a copy of Xavier Cugat's "Havana for a Night," which Dinah had mentioned to me she had cut on a one-side deal and which I knew was due for release. (She got $50 for the one shot.)

"Just got it in" smiled the clerk and reached into a box still unpacked.

Cooper flipped over Dinah's voice and interpretation of the lyric. I gave him her number so he could ask for permission to submit her for the job. He called and got it, made the submission, and she got the job. Then he told me what show was involved.

By the time the deal was set it already was old hat, so I didn't mention my part to Dinah. Whether Cooper ever told her how he became aware of her I don't know either.

I do know that several years later, after I'd been off *Variety* and hadn't seen Cooper for some time, I ran into him in the company of two high-level ad agency executives whom I knew. When he realized I was about to say hello he hurriedly walked right by.

The ironic part of Dinah's history is that she deliberately avoided working with a Big Band, from whence virtually every star solo singer of that time sprang. Yet, it was a recording with a big band that gave her the break she'd been awaiting.

Dinah made it big because she was then and always was a class act. She handled herself well and avoided the pitfalls that tripped up many a female vocal aspirant of that time. She persistently rejected jobs that did not appear to further her career. I recall Tommy Dorsey offering her a lot of money, for that time, to join his band. She turned him down.

In the late 30's and early 40's the competition was heavy. The spotlight was on the Big Bands and their featured singers. They were beacons that drew aspiring talent out of the woodwork of every part of the country.

Talent alone, however, was not always the answer. Breaks, good agents, good personal managers who could move mountains, or sometimes just good looks made successes out of performers that were not always the best performers. Conversely, many a good talent that had the best representation went down the drain or just existed in the gray area between solid success and going home to forget the whole thing.

Where show business is concerned, the old wheeze "cream always rises to the top" often is just a wheeze. Usually, the deterrent is a lack of spine, unwillingness to take the grind, inability to stomach the disappointments and frustrations that inevitably plague a newcomer.

And for a chick trying on the big town for size there was every kind of trap imaginable. Legions of low-level agents, managers, and con men lay in wait. These wolves had more ways to strip a kid of nest-egg money, earnings, or panties than a pickpocket.

And it was the earnest ones they loved to work over.

On the other hand there were legions of kids who'd made up their minds before the spires of Manhattan were in sight that they'd make it any way possible—on their backs or on their knees if not before an upright audition microphone. Hollywood also was inundated.

So the competition was really tough when Dinah challenged. And she kept it clean. At first the only ones aware of her great talent were the music publishers for whom she recorded audition disks of new songs, and trade paper men. But word slowly got around about her and she got better and better jobs.

One important showcase was a five-time-a-week radio broadcast spot on WNEW, New York. Bernice Judas, owner and operator of the station, was a good friend (she gave my wife and me a wedding present of an end table from W & J Sloane that we still have, 54 years later). Martin Block, WNEW's premier disk-jockey, and I often mentioned Dinah to Judas, but whether that helped I do not know. When Dinah got the job I was surprised.

I didn't see Dinah for years afterward. The last time was in the late 40's when she was doing a full-hour TV show out of Hollywood. I was on the Coast and having lunch with Dick Jacobs, former trombonist with Tommy Dorsey and then Tommy Dorsey's Hollywood music company rep. He was going to Dinah's rehearsal and suggested I go along.

Dinah was in the middle of a dress rehearsal and when she saw me in the wings she stopped everything, rushed over and hugged me, which was a no-no. You just don't stop dress-rehearsals.

I loved it.

Dinah's death in the spring of 1994 was a sad blow to me, even though I hadn't seen her for years. As I said, she was a class-act.

Patti Page

All writers on trade papers, who are much closer to their subjects than daily-paper reporters or columnists, at least once in their careers encountered a bandleader, singer, agency exec or promotion man with whom everything always went wrong.

For me it was Patti Page.

But, from her, I got many kicks.

Even from one of her songs. I was sound asleep at 2 a.m. in the old Sherman Hotel, Chicago, when a strange noise awakened me. Groggily, I sat up, listened for a few minutes, then rolled out laughing my head off.

My room was high in the bottom part of the U-shaped hotel, consequently sound was magnified. A bunch of high-living conventioneers on a lower floor were singing Patti's "Doggie In the Window." When they reached the "arf" line it seemed, from the

147

full sound, that someone in every room in that part of the hotel barked the response. What made the whole thing funnier was the "arf arfs" came in tempo and in close unison.

I had very little contact with Patti and none of it was pleasant. As a relative newcomer she debuted a soloist singing policy in the Terrace Room of the New Yorker Hotel, which till then had been a big band spot. Patti was obviously nervous and it showed. My review wasn't enthusiastic. While allowances can be made for opening-night jitters, a performer playing a major booking such as the Terrace Room is expected to be top-notch. And Patti was not.

She never forgot.

Patti's attitude notwithstanding, I have a very warm spot in my heart for her due to the treatment she gave Jack Rael, her manager over the years. In a business that too often works on the basis of "don't tell me what you did for me yesterday, tell me what you're doing for me today," Patti's conduct re Rael over the years was completely contrary to most artist-manager relationships.

Rael, a musician, arranger, and conductor, came across Patti when she was singing on a Tulsa, Oklahoma radio station and Rael, so the story goes, accidentally tuned to her program. A musician, he was in town with a traveling band.

Patti was singing for peanuts and living on the wrong side of the tracks. She required almost everything. Rael signed her to a contract, dressed her, trained her, selected songs, made arrangements, eventually got her a contract with Mercury Records and signed her to GAC, one of the major booking agencies of the time.

Rael devised the "voice-over" multi-track approach used for the first time on "Tennessee Waltz" and Patti was a star in short order.

Did she appreciate all that Rael did for her? You bet! Her response was to increase Rael's percentage of her earnings, according to a top GAC executive with whom I frequently golfed, to the point where Rael eventually owned 50 percent from the first dollar.

That sort of appreciation by an artist for a manager is unheard of, particularly after stardom is achieved. When they hit the top most performers will not permit themselves to believe that success is due to effort other than their own. And as a means of avoiding being constantly reminded of who was responsible for their new style of living, they often find an excuse to jettison the real cause.

Examples are legion. This is a minor one. On the recommendation of a GAC exec, I signed an act in 1957 consisting of three boys called The Tempos. They were working for peanuts. The act featured a lead singer whose voice came across like a calliope, much like the later Four Seasons.

I signed a conditional deal, predicated on my producing a record contract plus increasing their earnings before I took any income. I sold the act to a relatively small independent record label because I had confidence in owner Jack Gold, who later became head of all Columbia Record operations in Hollywood. Then we went looking for songs.

On a "park-ride" bus I used every day from New Jersey, I ran into songwriter Sherman Edwards (later to write the Broadway hit "1776"). He dug into his trunk and came up with a beautiful ballad titled "See You in September." It became a huge spring and summer hit, eventually selling over 600,000 copies, a tremendous sale for those times.

An example of artist loyalty (or lack of it) was shown me by a tremendous group called The Beachcombers, a combination of three boys and a Hawaiian girl. The act was drawing $700 weekly when they worked. I wrote a contract calling for me to provide them with a recording contract and to forego any commission until they were earning $1,000 weekly.

With GAC booking I kept them working. I arranged an RCA-Victor recording contract.

When Eddie Fisher came out of the Army he was discharged on a Tuesday. GAC, which handled him for theaters only, had him booked into the Paramount Theater, New York, then perhaps the premier theater date in the country. Realizing that virtually every important agency executive in all phases of show business would get to the Paramount to check out Fisher after his long stint in service, I sat on Harry Anger, GAC's theater booker, and succeeded in getting the 'Combers on the same bill. They did a great job.

A short time later Perry Como decided to rid himself of the troublesome Fontaine Sisters (whom I also managed until they drove me crazy). Tom Rockwell, owner and head of GAC, set up an audition for the Beachcombers, going to lengths I couldn't believe. He "borrowed" a nightclub on New York's East Side (La Vie En Rose), got a lighting man to stage it, brought in a group of musicians, and the act did its thing under ideal conditions.

It was a tremendous test and I felt we were "in like Flynn" until the advertising agency executives who represented Chesterfield, which sponsored Como and also Arthur Godfrey, decided that it was too risky for the client to back another "mixed" group. The girl in the Beachcombers, as I said, was Hawaiian and Chesterfield already had been receiving flack about Haleloke, the Hawaiian singer with Godfrey, and about The Mariners, also with Godfrey, which consisted of two black and two white men.

It was at this point I found that only the leader of the Beachcombers read music. He was the arranger. That fact would have made a spot with Como very difficult since he occasionally changed songs at the last minute and there would have been no time for the group to learn new material.

Then I booked the group into the Sands Hotel, Las Vegas. They drew double their salary in the Lounge. Since Las Vegas isn't exactly around the corner from New York I didn't get to hold their hands very often. They stopped paying me commissions (this after I had gotten the William Morris Agency to hold still for 5 percent commission because I had booked the date myself).

When they owed me $16,000, I sued and settled for less plus spending a goodly sum flying to Vegas with my New York attorney to press my case.

Here I suspect there was a joker in the woodpile. Bill Burton, my good "friend" from the Jimmy Dorsey days, was living in Vegas. He dug the 'Combers and sought to manage them. When he found that I handled their affairs he called me and asked to buy their contract. I refused.

Since I was in New York and the act was in Las Vegas I didn't see them often. Telephone and mail were our only contact for several months. Burton subtly began working on them about their absentee manager and stirred them up sufficiently that they breached their contract with me.

They signed with Burton. He booked the group into a Reno casino after closing the Sands. Driving north in the early morning, their vehicle went out of control, flew off the road into the desert, flipping several times. One of the group was killed and others badly injured. They never worked together again.

Tales such as the above are not the exception in show business, they are the norm. Artists and their managers are not always on the same track, especially after success is attained.

But, to get back to Patti. As I said, I have the greatest admiration for the gal because of the way she handled her relationship with Rael. But, I seemed unable to avoid getting into trouble with her and her entourage.

In the spring of 1951 I booked the Ralph Flanagan band into the Lyric Theater, Indianapolis, for a week to be played the following September at a price of $12,500, plus a percentage over a certain figure. The contract required us to bring with us a fairly good supporting act.

Reading *Billboard*, I noticed a new recording by Patti rising on the charts, titled "Tennessee Waltz." I contacted GAC, which also booked Flanagan, and bought Patti for $2,000 for the September week. Remember, this was spring.

By the time the theater date rolled around "Tennessee Waltz" had become a smash hit and Patti's theater price had jumped from $2,000 to $5,000. As a result, Rael insisted the Lyric contract be rewritten to increase Patti's base salary and that she participate in the overage, if there was any.

I refused. I pointed out that I had bought Patti five months before and if "Tennessee Waltz" had dropped dead instead of becoming a smash hit we would still have honored the contract. Besides which, I pointed out to Rael, he wasn't too smart in booking that far ahead when he had a potential smash recording climbing the charts. Or did he do it deliberately, figuring I would cave in under his and GAC's pressure when the date came up and the record was a hit?

In short, did he plan to have his cake and eat it too?

As it turned out it perhaps would have been better to rewrite the contract and give Patti more of her due. The week was chaos.

Patti did everything she could to screw things up and Flanagan, a nasty bastard anyhow, matched her move for move.

It was a week's work one tried to forget.

CHAPTER 19

Doris Day

There were a lot of phonies in the music business back then and I knew most of them.

A newspaperman, especially in show business, is a target for every con man in town.

Most were press agents, others were song pluggers, and still others were booking agents.

Some, like Marty Melcher, were masters at the con.

"If I can't make it myself, I'll marry it," vowed the tall, dark, and handsome Melcher, whom I then knew only slightly, as a song plugger for the firms owned by Lou Levy, the manager of the Andrews Sisters.

The scene was Levy's music publishing offices in Radio City.

Melcher was from Cleveland, Ohio, where he promoted songs for Levy. He was the epitome of the tall-dark-and-handsome and he knew it well. He had an ego a mile wide and a nasty disposition to match, which is why I didn't know him too well.

I took a dim view of him and avoided him whenever I could.

The art of plugging songs had a pecking order and the art of ass-kissing was fine-tuned at every level. Those at the top, usually personality-plus exuders, be they owners, professional managers, or everyday song pluggers, were often well respected and important to bandleaders and solo singers with a recording contract, because these men were in close contact with songwriters, therefore in a position to come up at any time with a new song—a potential hit.

Melcher was a song plugger and he apparently suffered it as a means to a better end.

The "end" arrived in the late 40's. The Andrews Sisters at that point were top level stars and their selling price to theaters was so high that they could not work as an individual act in conjuction with a Big Band. Therefore they had to "own" the entire presentation.

Levy put together a complete package starring the Andrews plus one or two acts he bought, and backed the whole thing with an orchestra conducted by Mitch Ayres, then at loose ends following the demise of his own orchestra and before Perry Como.

The final touch was to add Melcher as "Road Manager." Melcher wasted no time. Patti Andrews wasn't married. Melcher took dead aim and in the space of the six or eight weeks the package was on the road, he had Patti's head spinning. She was the focal point of the Andrews trio and already a very wealthy gal. She succumbed to Melcher's blandishments and at the end of the tour they were married.

Patti was in seventh heaven. She and Melcher settled in the Hollywood area, where each of the Andrews girls owned a home.

For a long time the marriage seemed idyllic. But Melcher apparently was looking for even greener fields.

By this time Columbia Records had signed Doris Day as the result of her vocal of "Sentimental Journey" with Les Brown's Orchestra. Harry Mayer, the New York talent vocal scout for Warner Brothers, signed her to a film contract. She arrived in Hollywood to begin her long and illustrious career.

Melcher knew Doris from his song plugging contacts with Brown while working for Levy. To start with, she was a much more delectable dish than Patti and, with any luck, figured to become a bigger star. Warner Brothers had big plans for her.

Melcher revised his sights and took dead aim on Doris, while he was still married to Patti.

Melcher began staying out late, at first. Then started an all-night routine. His new alliance permeated Hollywood gossip. Patti, genuinely in love with him, went berserk. According to the stories that seeped east she would drive to Doris's house in the wee hours, pound on the door and demand Melcher come home. She tried everything to keep the home fires burning, to no avail. Melcher divorced Patti and immediately married Doris. The rest of the story Doris tells in her book, written in the late 70's.

Melcher apparently took over every aspect of "Operation Doris." He negotiated contracts, handled her money, and even adopted her son by her first marriage to trombonist Taft Jordan. They lived on a ranch. Raised horses—the whole ball of wax.

Every time I saw the credits on a new Doris Day picture, citing Melcher as "Producer," Lorraine had to stop me from guffawing out loud. The guy didn't have a brain in his tall, dark, and handsome body. But, he had balls, and he was smart enough, or stupid enough, whichever way one looks at it, to slowly loot Doris' finances, in cahoots with an attorney.

After Melcher died at a relatively young age Doris discovered the evaporation of her cash via Melcher's manipulations. She sued Melcher's estate and the attorney, and eventually recovered some $6,000,000.

Browsing through Doris' book, I got quite a shock. There was never a word in the music business while Doris was with Les Brown that she was addicted to any sex. She looked like a cold-ass chick to me. As a rule, any music biz female who liked to spend time on her back or on her knees sooner or later became a known quantity.

Not so with Doris.

CHAPTER 20

The Andrews Sisters

I've mentioned Juggy Gayle and the role he played in opening doors for me soon after I started gathering music news for *Variety*. He was one of the most enthusiastic denizens of the music publishing industry and well known to virtually everyone.

A few days after we met in the spring of 1938, Juggy towed me to an apartment above a Woolworth's store on Sixth Avenue (now Avenue of the Americas) between 56th and 57th. As we entered, I heard a strange but appealing song being wailed by three uniformly unattractive girls gathered around a piano being played by a thin, goose-necked character who didn't say much. The whole scene was dominated by a short, owlish-looking man who never stopped moving or issuing orders.

The trio was the then-unknown Andrews Sisters. The pianist was Saul Chaplin and the dominant one was a fledgling songwriter named Sammy Cahn. He and Chaplin had adapted an old Jewish melody and called it "Bei Mir Bist Du Schoen." The trio was to record the song in a few days for Decca Records.

The apartment belonged to Lou Levy, the trio's manager, a semi-professional dancer. Levy, Juggy, Cahn, and Chaplin were all from Brooklyn and were pushing each other's talents. Levy had only recently come across the trio, fresh out of Minneapolis, and had gotten them a contract to record for Decca.

An excellent promoter, Levy had worked out a deal with Martin Block, then the New York area's premier disk-jockey, to debut the recording on his Sunday morning broadcast from the Criterion Theater, on Times Square, before a huge live audience. Usually, his disk jockey shows were done from his WNEW studios on Madison Avenue, in the original CBS building.

Block was a power unparalleled to this day among New York jockeys. When he liked something he gave it his best shot. And he went for "Bei Mir." He promoted it into an instant hit, and the girls were off and running. In those days, a single hit recording could "make" an artist.

The record quickly became the No. 1 best-seller, setting the trio's hooks into bundles and bundles of coin and eventually establishing them as one of the greatest female singing groups of all time. Patti, Maxine, and Laverne, however, made no bones about the fact that their work was patterned after their idols, the Boswell Sisters, the first and greatest female trio. After the Andrews came the McGuire Sisters. Each trio had a different sound. Each was tremendously successful.

I got to know the girls fairly well. They were as different as three sisters could possibly be. Patti, very outgoing, devil-may-care. Laverne, quiet and unassuming. Maxene was the main gear

When the Music Stopped

THE BIG BAND ERA REMEMBERED

FRANK SINATRA, Bernie Woods, Barry Gray (at mike).

A MIDNIGHT BROADCAST AT WOR: Henny Youngman, unidentified, Frank Sinatra, Bernie Woods, Jo Stafford, Perry Como, Barry Gray (at mike).

AT MEADOWBROOK: unidentified, Barry Gray, Mitch Ayres, Bernie Woods, Tommy Valando, unidentified, Randy Brooks.

THE EVERY DAY FOURSOME: George Paxton, Mitch Ayres, Bernie Woods, Tommy Valando.

SAMMY KAYE, Barry Gray, Chuck Foster, Bernie Woods, Mickey Glass, Randy Brooks, Woody Herman.

OWNER OF Narragansett Race Track, Buddy Clark, Bernie Woods, Lou Mindling.

MOB SCENE at Fred Waring's Shawnee on the Delaware before Music Men's Annual Golf Tourney. Waring is reading *Variety*. Bernie Woods is at his left.

JOE SHRIBMAN, Mitch Ayres, Bernie Woods, Joe Galkin.

FRANK SINATRA, Bernie Woods, Jo Stafford, Perry Como, Barry Gray.

STEVE YATES, Charlie Yates, Bernie Woods, unidentified, Manie Sachs, Abe Olman, Cork O'Keefe.

AT FRED WARING'S Shawnee on the Delaware: Perry Como (with cigarette), Bernie Woods (fourth from the left), and a group of music publishers.

and handled most of the trio's business dealings with Levy, whom she eventually married. And she drove a car like a racer, which got my attention.

Levy used the recording power of the trio and the money he made with the group to establish a music publishing empire. He formed strong overseas connections and came up with hit after hit. Songs like "Gypsy" and "Galway Bay" to cite just a couple, made hundreds of thousands for his firms.

Levy did not expand, however, in the area of artists' management. He may have signed an act or two here and there for a specific purpose, but never seriously got into that aspect. Any other manager I knew, including myself, would have used the power of the Andrews group to sign other performers with potential and force them into positions, using the girls as a lever, that could polish their stars.

Lou made it plain his groove was publishing. He firmly believed in the line he used to throw out, seconded, I imagine, by any other artist-manager.

He'd say he intended to write a book, the title would be "Copyrights Don't Talk Back."

I have another strong recollection about Levy and it arises often when I hear certain songs or run into someone like Sammy Cahn, as I did a while back when we both were running across Avenue of Americas in different directions to beat a traffic light. Sammy, whom I hadn't noticed, grabbed me in mid-street and we both almost got nailed by a fast-starting cab.

Sammy, who recently passed away, was one of the greatest song-writing talents ever to hit Tin Pan Alley. His hits, many written for films, are legion. But, more importantly, he was a great guy. He had a tremendous drive to succeed, even after he succeeded.

A Gary Cooper in appearance he was not, but he became a Broadway attraction when he conducted a one-man show based on his musical accomplishments

One evening back before "Bei Mir" was released and long before the good things happened, Lou invited me and Juggy to dinner. We met at a French restaurant near his apartment. Also present were Sammy and Saul Chaplin; Jimmy Van Heusen, then a $60-a-week accompanist at Remick Music, but also a budding songwriter who had just written "Pennies from Heaven" and who later penned many of the great songs recorded by Bing Crosby; Howie Richmond, who later managed The Weavers and, using them as a base, built a tremendous music publishing empire of his own. (He had been in Lou's apartment the day I first met the Andrews trio.)

The point of all this is that when we were finished with dinner, this group, every member of which later became a millionaire (with the exception of Juggy and me) couldn't pay the check. Levy thought he had enough cash, but didn't come close. After everyone turned out their pockets there still was not enough to spring us.

Levy got on the phone with Happy Goday, another West New York compatriot then working for Sunshine Biscuits in Long Island City, New York, who later became a major figure in publishing, to come bail us out.

From that "Bei Mir" beginning, Levy built an empire that he eventually sold to Metromedia for a reported $4,500,000. He and his wife went to England and Levy managed to blow the whole wad. He came back to the United States and went to work for Tommy Valando, who had previously sold his own publishing combine to Metromedia for the same "reported" amount of $4,500,000, plus a healthy contract to manage.

CHAPTER 21

Vaughn Monroe

The big band era did not feature many good singing leaders. Vaughn Monroe, whether you liked his approach to pop songs or didn't, was a very unusual entry.

I like him personally and his work. It was different. And it resulted in a number of hit recordings which made the band a solid money-maker.

The last time I saw Vaughn was a most unlikely accidental meeting. I was running a division of Enoch Light's Command Records, subsidiary of American Broadcasting Corporation, and was in Chicago for meetings with the Webcor Company, then perhaps the largest manufacturer of tape machines—the old fashioned reel-to-reel kind.

Walking up Michigan Ave. at 7 a.m. toward the Chicago-Sheraton, I noticed a disreputable-looking character leaning against the hotel's canopy pole. As I got closer I thought the figure looked familiar. Then I was sure I knew the "bum."

A familiar voice boomed, "Bernie Woods—what the hell are you doing on Michigan Avenue at 7 a.m. of a Saturday morning?" The voice was unmistakable behind the two-day beard. The beat-up old cap and well-worn jacket were Vaughn Monroe's flying clothes. He and his wife Marion were on the way to a Las Vegas booking.

We had a great old time rehashing the early days of his career and the furor his voice caused, pro and con. We laughed over the time he was booked into the Strand Theater, Brooklyn, which then was running big band shows in conjunction with the Strand Theater, on Broadway, both Warner Bros. houses. *Variety's* Abel Green, my boss, did not assign me to cover the show. Instead, at a whim, he sent the paper's "concert biz expert" (a Harvard grad who had a tough time finding his way to Brooklyn and back) to review Vaughn and his band. Abel was intrigued by Vaughn's unusual pipes and suggested the reviewer try to judge his singing from a concert, or classical, viewpoint.

The decision: "a classical voice with great concert potential."

Vaughn had called me and howled. He didn't agree with the evaluation and wouldn't kid himself.

Vaughn and I talked for a couple of hours (I blew my ten o'clock plane reservation and had a terrible time getting home). I thoroughly enjoyed the hours spent with him. He was one band-leader who knew where he was and where he was going. He had a refreshing, wry sense of humor.

Little did I know it would be the last time I'd ever see him. He died extremely young without enjoying the fruits of his successful show-business labors, but left his family well off. He had become part owner of The Meadows, a Boston suburb big band type of club similar to Frank Dailey's Meadowbrook. He owned a fleet of taxicabs in Boston itself, among other ventures.

Monroe was the first talent selection by Willard Alexander, after he left MCA to build a big band division for the William Morris Agency. When Willard mentioned Vaughn to me as his first project for Morris and played me a demo record of Vaughn's voice and trumpet playing, I was surprised. Alexander was the early-day champion of Benny Goodman at MCA. I had assumed he would go after a Benny Goodman-type band to kick things off for Morris. His selection of Vaughn was a distinct shock.

Nevertheless, via judicious management and an astute selection of material for RCA-Victor, Vaughn in time became one of the top money-makers in the music business.

That was the name of the game.

CHAPTER 22

Lionel Hampton

I saw Lionel Hampton a short while ago on a televised appearance from Washington, D.C. White-haired, in tails, he was the perfect representative bandleader at a time when modern "talent" seems to think it proper to appear before an audience in cut-offs and ragged shirts.

Lionel was another great musician I didn't know too well, had met only a few times. But it was easy to develop tremendous respect for his talent. I first heard him with Benny Goodman and later reviewed his exciting big band on a number of occasions.

"Hamp" was married back in the 40's to a woman named Gladys who dominated him and the band with a heavy hand. Joe Glaser, head of Associated Booking Corp., which handled Hampton's bookings, was himself a forceful character who strongly dominated his own sphere of operation. But he got nowhere with Gladys. She ran Lionel and the band with an iron grip that Glaser could not penetrate.

Gladys handled all the band's finances, collected monies due, paid the musicians, forwarded commissions, and paid all Lionel's living expenses.

Lionel didn't have to do a thing, except perform. For that he received very little. It was a standing gag among his musicians that none would ever lend him money. If they did, the chances were they'd never get it back. Gladys gave Lionel an allowance of $5.00 a week and, once it was gone, he'd be dead until the following week.

Meanwhile, according to Glaser, Gladys owned a half dozen fur coats, traveled behind the band on the road in a Cadillac, her only companion the band's boy singer. Lionel rode the bus.

When she died, relatively young, a key was found among her effects, which turned out to fit a safe deposit box in a New York bank. The box contained over $160,000 in cash. The bank records showed she hadn't been near the box in quite some time.

My wildest recollection of Lionel I remember to this day. His band opened at the Apollo Theater in Harlem. I was assigned to the review. When I reached the theater there didn't seem to be a seat in the house. However, the theater's manager, Mr. Franklin, a most accommodating man, found an empty seat in the very center of the first row of the balcony.

It was a beautiful location to see the show—until Lionel kicked off his famed "Flying Home" arrangement. The reaction of the fans to the beat of the band made the balcony jump. It literally bounced to the band's beat. It scared me so much I jumped up, worked my way into the aisle (which wasn't easy), and caught the rest of the show from downstairs, behind the orchestra section seats.

CHAPTER 23

Bobby Byrne

In all my years of reporting news and reviewing talent for *Variety*, the first and only time I ever thought I was going to be physically assaulted for anything I wrote was in 1940 following a review of the then-new Bobby Byrne Orchestra.

Bobby Byrne was a trombonist from Detroit, originally a replacement in Jimmy Dorsey's Orchestra for brother Tommy Dorsey.

He was blonde, good-looking, and tremendously talented in a great many directions, but was his own worst enemy. He was a standout on trombone, as he had to be to replace Tommy, but he had the personality of an asp. He consistently rubbed people the wrong way.

Bobby became a bandleader after several years as a sideman with Jimmy when General Artists Corporation (Jimmy's reps) put up the money to get him started. GAC felt he could be developed into a rival trombonist-leader to Tommy.

As a musician within a group, Byrne was an outstanding performer. As a bandleader he was something else. His superior trombone talent for the most part made beautiful solo sounds. But too often he'd stumble over lip or tongue and make himself look like a kid trying the horn on for size.

A martinet, Byrne was thoroughly disliked by most of his own men. He had an ego as wide as a boulevard. Woe betide the musician or any person he had control over who disagreed with his opinions.

The new Bobby Byrne Orchestra made its major debut at the Glen Island Casino, New Rochelle, New York, a major booking for an established band, let alone a new one. The launching gave the new band an outstanding start and tremendous national notice since the Casino originated a number of network radio broadcasts, the lifeblood of the big band business. It had a reputation as one of the "makers" of new bands. (Glenn Miller really kicked into the big time via a summer-long booking there in 1940.)

Byrne's band was not a very cohesive unit when I reviewed its performance a few days after opening and Bobby, through nervousness or frustration or whatever, strove too hard on his horn and "goofed" a lot.

My review of the band was not very complimentary (which put me into the doghouse with Tom Rockwell, head of GAC, major owner of the agency, and a valued friend).

A few weeks later I went back to Glen Island to give the band another hearing and possibly a follow-up review. When Bobby saw me enter he promptly jumped off the bandstand and came hustling over. His physical attitude told me that one wrong word out of me and I'd be slugged. I'm sure the only thing that stopped him was the fact that, as a *Variety* reporter, I and the sheet could retaliate in so many different ways.

Since Byrne's new band was backed by GAC, which meant some of the band industry's most powerful figures were involved, he got every opportunity a leader could possibly receive. The band was booked into every major build-up spot in the country— Frank Dailey's Meadowbrook, The Strand theater, New York, Palladium Ballroom, Hollywood, then the outstanding West Coast booking. And it got beaucoup air-time from every stop. Yet, the band failed.

Byrne later joined the Air Force and became a P-38 Lightning pilot. To my knowledge he never got overseas (he joined so late), but I have no doubt that had he gotten into World War II in any theater he would have given a great account of himself.

I didn't see Byrne for years after I left *Variety* and went into the management business (even though he was a sideman in the Mitch Ayres Orchestra, which backed Perry Como's TV broadcasts and I very often visited the originating studio). Then I gave up management (rock was rearing its ugly head) and joined Enoch Light to develop a new division of his Command Records.

On the first day Enoch piloted me around the office to meet the staff. I almost fell down when the first person I met was Byrne, who was Enoch's assistant in planning recording dates, hiring musicians, and performing a major amount of the studio work in the production of the company's then high-selling LP's. He was cordial, but obviously had not forgotten me.

Several years later, Enoch did not renew his contract and left ABC to establish another new record company. Loren Becker, Command's sales manager, a singer with Enoch's original band and another dilly of an egotist, was named by ABC to replace him and Byrne became his assistant. I mention this only by way of pointing out an incident that explains Byrne in the best way possible.

I can't remember the contents of the memo I wrote to Becker, with a copy to Byrne. But, when Byrne received the memo from his secretary in the middle of a recording date at studios that were extremely expensive, Byrne stopped the costly activity and called me to advise me that the memo I wrote to Becker should have been directed to him, with a copy to Becker.

Since he was not my boss I told him to where to stick what and hung up. I could not believe anyone could be such an asshole.

When it came time for Becker to leave the company because his ego and lack of know-how caused the Command line to decline in sales, Byrne helped Becker clean out his large office and commiserated with him all the way to the elevator. When the doors closed, he high-tailed it into the office of President Larry Newton, to explain that the fall of Command was all Becker's fault, that he had disagreed with Becker's policies and tactics all along, but had been overruled and forced to accept the ideas that had proved so unsuccessful.

Newton couldn't wait to tell Charley Trepel, Command sales manager, and me about Byrne's "fidelity" to Becker.

Then I recalled that Newton's own business policies were not much above that level. I once paid him over $600 to underwrite a recording date for an independent record label then owned by Newton, using the Tommy Reynolds Orchestra, featured on WOR Radio, and which I managed.

About six months later the American Federation of Musicians threatened me with loss of my manager's license unless I came up forthwith with the money due the Reynolds musicians. Luckily, I still had the canceled check I had given Newton to cover all costs and on it had noted exactly what it covered.

CHAPTER 24

The Critics

Even though I was one, albeit part time, some of my best laughs have come from the writings of so-called "professional" critics.

This subject came to mind via a column I read in the *San Francisco Examiner* late in 1993, combined with a recollection of a similar writing for *Variety* while I was Music Editor.

The *Examiner* critic tore apart and booted from goalpost to goalpost Barbra Streisand's latest album "Back to Broadway." I have not heard the release in its entirety—only a couple of tracks on radio programs—but this critic's comments were so obvious it was laughable.

One of the oldest wheezes among critics is to pick out someone in the spotlight and rap them to kingdom come. Pay no attention to the fact that what you might be rapping has been a star for many years based on proven talent. Lay in wait until you think

173

they've made even the slightest mistake, then jump on them publicly with both feet. You might be noticed. You might become a local celebrity. And someone in the "big city" might take notice.

Based on the three or four tracks I did hear and being familiar with Streisand's past performances, I know there is no way she could take standards, great songs from various Broadway musicals, and do as bad a job on them as this guy claimed. His stupid criticisms apparently did not help. He's still in San Francisco.

In the late 40's I was going on vacation from my *Variety* post. Since I wrote weekly record reviews, my boss asked me what I thought of the idea of a guest columnist for the two issues I would be away. I agreed. He therefore contacted a critic on the *Boston Globe*. Weeks later, the *Globe* man sent in his first column and Abel handed it to me to edit.

I could not believe what I was reading. Like the *Examiner* expert, this boy apparently had ideas. He selected Bing Crosby, still one of the biggest stars anywhere. And what he did to the Groaner's talent in 15 or 20 inches of type was hard to fathom and hard to believe. As they say in the lower regions, "He cut Bing a new-ass," with deep slices so vicious the intent was obvious.

Given the fact that Crosby perhaps was wearing a bit, he still did not deserve what this guy obviously enjoyed writing. It stuck out that here was a nondescript writer trying to wangle a reputation.

I told Abel I was returning the column to Boston. We argued. My departure was imminent and there wasn't time to dig up a replacement. Besides which, I suspect, Abel had some kind of a mad on against Jack Kapp, head of Decca (Bing's label), one of his oldest friends. He ordered me to let the column run.

Lindy's buzzed about the uncalled for rap. Before the week was out, this guy was in town on a couple of interviews. Apparently, they didn't work out. He was still on the *Globe* when he died.

Being a critic is not easy, but it's not as difficult as it may seem. There are three possible reactions to any show or performance and the critic always has two of the three going for him, or her, every time out:

1. A review is a snap to write if the subject is from good to sensational.
2. A review is a snap if the subject is poor to very bad.
3. A review is very difficult to write if the subject is middle-of-the-road, neither good nor bad.

The in-between performances are the ones that syphon the blood from a dedicated reviewer's veins.

Luckily, most critics seem to take their tasks seriously. It's not often one reads a rap with a self-aggrandizing purpose, but they usually are easy to spot. And not all critics are accurate, despite their reputations and the sheets they work for. The drama critic of the *New York Times* rapped "Oklahoma" when it opened on Broadway, to cite one of the classic goofs of "professional" critics.

The only thing a critic can do to assure himself he's at least trying to do a job is simply to sit back and wait for his own reactions to any performance. And he or she does not have to be fully experienced in any particular area to give a reaction to something seen or heard.

The problems arise when a critic "leans forward" intent on finding something to criticize.

Plus which any critic in any area of entertainment can always bank on the real fact that a majority of new Broadway shows, new record releases, new films, or new anything are destined for the bone yard. Less than 40 percent of anything new in the entertainment world reaches hit status.

That's a proven statistic.

Gene Krupa

It was a bit early in my *Variety* career when Gene Krupa left Benny Goodman to launch his own band. But the advent of that band and the varied reaction to it by two prominent contacts helped me immeasurably in my thinking about the job that had been dropped into my lap.

Gene debuted the new band at a New Jersey ballroom with a network broadcast, a most unusual way to kick off a new outfit. Usually, a "first-date" was a "shakedown" cruise—without anything as revealing as a radio wire. The wire was arranged for Krupa's debut because there was so much interest. His tenure with Goodman had focused a great deal of attention on him.

John Hurley, whom I have said was writing music news before I came into the music picture, was assigned to review the band at the ballroom. But I heard the broadcast and formed a few opinions, perhaps unfairly, because for many reasons (mike placement, for one) a broadcast is not always to be trusted.

The next day I sought out Arthur Michaud's opinion. He was the band's manager and had every reason to laud its performance. But Arthur was an honest man. He didn't like what he had heard on the first performance.

I then went to see Willard Alexander. He had been against Gene leaving Benny and going out on his own. Since MCA was booking Gene, he had good reason to laud the band, but I knew he was honest. And he thought the band was great.

I chewed on the two reactions for a bit and came to the conclusion that, if two prominent and very experienced band men came to different opinions of the same subject, that meant only one thing:

My opinion was as good as theirs.

From that point on I never worried about what anyone else thought of what I wrote in a review, no matter what the subject. It changed my whole approach to the job. I became much more positive and confident.

Krupa, of course, went on to become a big factor in the big band scene. I didn't always agree with the arranging for the band, but the performance was outstanding. It featured great "spotlight" musicians in trumpeter Roy Eldridge, saxist Charlie Ventura, and clarinet/sax man Buddy DeFranco. Gene recorded a number of great sides for Columbia Records, among them "Drumboogie" and "Let Me Off Uptown."

As I may have said before, I didn't know Gene personally very well—until I joined the recording division of American Broadcasting Company (Command). At least two or three days a week I and a couple co-workers would lunch at the Carnegie Deli at 55th and Seventh Ave. in New York. There I ran into Gene almost every visit and he would sit with us and talk. Through these frequent conversations I got to know him well (he was living in Yonkers, New York with old friend Jack Egan, Tommy Dorsey's former publicity man).

His death was a sad day for the music business.

Louis Prima

Most of the successes among the Big Bands were due to leaders' being great instrumentalists. Rarely did a leader pop up with natural comic tendencies, which heightened his impact.

Louis Prima was a standout in this area.

Prima was one the prime nuts of the band business, but an immensely likable one. And he led a very acceptable band.

Being Italian, Prima struck a mother lode of recorded hits featuring Italian-styled songs.

On the bandstand, Louis was a wild performer, one of the very best in getting an audience "up" and keeping it alive. He was showmanship personified, sometimes a bit crude, but nevertheless a great audience-pleaser. And his band's exciting arrangements backed his wild, strong trumpet-playing and his sometimes crude vocals.

Prima's success also laid bare for him a mother-lode of sex from gals of all ages. Frank Dailey, whose Meadowbrook Prima often played, once mentioned to me that he was sure Louis had laid every waitress that ever worked his place. And the place was sizable.

While Louis was a top-notch womanizer his methods surpassed most other bandleaders although he didn't always chase his own pussy. He himself told me of one of his ways of gathering feminine playthings: He'd look over a crowd of dancers, note a particularly delectable one, and point her out to his girl vocalist. They'd both watch and when the objective went to the ladies' room the vocalist would follow and talk to the girl about meeting Louis and possibly going out with him. Louis gathered a number of conquests that way although he normally needed nobody's help in reaping feminine talent. He was an avid head-hunter.

Like Tommy Dorsey, Louis also carried his sex within the band just to avoid barren nights. He had one really capable vocalist who was a nympho. She occasionally would help Louis' bookings along by keeping agents and bookers happy.

Louis invested his money in various ways, one of them extremely surprising to me when I learned of it—race horses. One night at Meadowbrook he mentioned he wasn't going to sleep that night, he was headed for Belmont Race Track, on Long Island, perhaps seventy miles away. I naturally came back with, "The first race isn't until one o'clock."

"Nah," he said, "I'm going for the early morning workouts. I own a couple horses and I like to see them run."

That floored me. Prima didn't seem the type. When I recovered I told him that my family, way back, was involved in racing, in Canada. My grandfather, a feisty Irishman who weighed less than a bag of feed, had been a jockey, and my father an exercise boy. I had been aimed that way when a youngster at fourteen weighing 98 pounds but, following a serious illness, had ballooned to 123 and was out of contention.

From that time on, much to my wife's dismay, I'd rise at 3:30 a.m. of a Wednesday or Thursday morning, if Louis was in town, and I'd meet him at the workouts. If it were Wednesday, my day off, I'd then head for the golf course. (As I've said often, it's a wonder I'm still married after 54 years.)

Prima called me one day and said that a two-year-old he had recently bought was entered in a race at Aqueduct and that he'd likely go off at fancy odds. He felt the colt had a great shot on the basis of workout times. He suggested I meet him and we might clean up.

The two-year-old looked great in the pre-race parade. He was on the board at 35-to-1. The horses entered the gate. When it was sprung I had my glasses on the colt. He stumbled. That was that.

"Bucked his shins," said Prima (kicked himself), while I watched $100 across go down the drain.

The last time I was in Las Vegas a friend I ran into mentioned Louis had a business on the outskirts of town. (I vaguely recollect it was a short golf course.) My wife and I drove out to see him, only to find he was away. Not too long after, he fell ill and passed away.

He was one the Big Band Era's memorable characters.

CHAPTER 27

Guy Lombardo

Pop band leaders of the "Era," most relatively young, were superfast at sniffing out sex.

If it were not handed to them on a silver platter they found little difficulty running it down themselves.

Of all the leaders of the time, however, the most unlikely at sexual didoes was a leader whose band was constantly castigated by critics and rivals.

But he and his brother were playtime champs.

Their names were Guy and Carmen Lombardo.

They were bulls.

Sex-wise, Guy and Carmen quietly made rival leaders look like high-school boys. They had society matrons and others patiently waiting for "Auld Lang Syne" on any given evening at the Roosevelt Grill, the band's annual winter booking.

Neither brother seemed that masculine. Guy's conducting style was somewhat effeminate-looking and Carmen's vocalizing and his way of handling instrumental solos seemed equally suspicious.

But, off the bandstand, sex was their forte.

Carmen was for years enamored of the wife of a high-ranking music man, who himself had outside interests. They apparently had an agreement. It was said, in those times, that Carmen and the wife would occupy one bedroom in the music man's apartment while the latter and his gal were in another.

Guy's hobby was well known; it was speed-boat (thunder-boats) racing. Hardly a play-time endeavor of anyone other than a complete man.

Guy's orchestra was for years the most successful of the sweet bands. Its style was instantly recognizable to fans, who obviously paid no attention to the fact that its output was criticized and vilified. It was one of the most successful sweet bands in the history of the band business.

New Year's Eve hasn't been the same since Guy's death.

There were four Lombardo brothers: Guy, Carmen, Victor (who for a time tried with his own band), and Leibert. The latter was the last to survive, until February, 1994.

CHAPTER 28

Buddy Rich

No big band ever succeeded without a standout drummer. There were many behind the bands of the Era, black and white, and many became stars in their own right, with their own bands or jazz combos.

Among the very best, if not the best of all, was a former juvenile star in his groove. His name was Buddy Rich.

Rich was fast—very. A fast mouth, too. But one hell of a musician.

I react to drums more than any other instrument. And Rich turned me on like a tall, slender anything. I have an extremely clear recollection of the guy under two different circumstances; both occurred many years ago but the pictures are no dimmer.

The most memorable is a Norman Granz "Jazz at the Philharmonic" concert at Carnegie Hall.

Before the start, I went backstage and among others saw
Buddy. He had the flu and was as sick as could be. His nose was
running, he had a temperature and he was miserable. No one
could have faulted him for defaulting. After all, how can a drummer work his skins and wipe his schnozz at the same time?

As sick as he was, Rich put on a solo demonstration of drum
mastery that literally stood my hair on end. He took off on one solo
that was unbelievable. The man unquestionably was the greatest
I've ever heard despite the fact that he came up in an era that produced tremendous skin talent—Sidney Catlett, Davey Tough,
Gene Krupa, Don Lamont, and others, all huge personalities
behind a set of skins.

None were Buddy's equal.

The second circumstance under which Rich impressed me
deeply was after he had launched his own band, which Frank
Sinatra is said to have backed with $25,000, despite the fact that
when both were with Tommy Dorsey they were always on the
verge of fisticuffs.

At any rate, Buddy's band was booked into New York's
Paramount, the premier theater booking in the entire country. I
can't recall how, but Buddy came up with a broken left arm or
wrist just before the opening. He showed up for rehearsal with the
arm in a cast.

That's akin to the proverbial one-armed paper-hanger.

But Rich carried it off, in the process showing a side of his
talent not often seen. The word for him until then was "attack."
With the cast, he showed superbly a new dimension: finesse. I
wrote in my review (I didn't have to look it up, I clearly remember) that "Rich plays as much drums with one arm as he does normally with two, by rechannelling his talent." And "Rich winds up
playing more with one arm than most of his cohorts do with two."

As for Buddy's big mouth, which frequently got him into trouble, I don't believe he meant or even considered half the things he blurted out. They marked him as a cocky, arrogant master of the snide remark. I probably am one of the few guys who never claimed to be present when he and Sinatra got into it back of the Astor Hotel bandstand, ostensibly because Rich was deliberately screwing up Frank's backgrounds.

The last time I saw Buddy work was accidental. I was in Chicago on business and found the band was at Mr. Kelly's, a popular spot on Rush Street, near Northside. His group was great although I could have been rolling in nostalgia. But, it pleased me greatly to see this as one of the few organized outfits still working.

And Buddy had not lost much, if any, of his touch.

CHAPTER 29

Richard Himber

One of the weirdest but most likable characters I came across while on *Variety* was a bandleader from before my time named Richard Himber.

He had previously been a fairly big name heading a sweet band that played New York hotels and many commercial network radio broadcasts, but was then not doing much musically. He had become more involved with magic, mind reading, and thought-transference.

Somehow Richard heard that at earlier times I had participated in exhibition matches on a pooltable against world-championship contenders. Though I did not at the time know him well, he called me and invited me to play. He wouldn't let up. I'd return to the office in late afternoon after a day seeking news and there would be three or four messages from Richard.

I usually worked Sunday afternoons writing and editing correspondents' copy. Richard got hip to that and often came pounding on the locked *Variety* street door, hoping to induce me to play. He even gifted me with a special cue.

Richard was a nice guy and, since I did like to play, I frequently accommodated him. But, by consistently beating him I made the situation worse. Until he turned to English snooker to try to get even. He did.

Richard was no fool. He was widely known in the magic circles of the time and had invented some tricks. When he had some new ones he'd invite me to dinner at his apartment at New York's Essex House Hotel, and try them out on me, while his seven-year old son whispered to me how they were performed.

On mind reading he'd pull things that flabbergasted me, although I was always suspicious of some sort of a gimmick. For example, he'd walk some fifty feet away, then ask that a phone number be written on a slip of paper and that you think of it. He would then repeat the number to you.

The first time he did it with me I'd written a number that had been assigned to me for a new house my wife and I were moving into two weeks hence. He repeated it perfectly.

Richard would call me at the office or home and do things over the phone like asking that I select a card, shuffle the deck then turn the cards over one at a time. He'd let me go three cards past the one selected then say, "Stop, go back three."

Russ Case, arranger and conductor, whom I managed later, told me of a time he was playing in a commercial radio band conducted by Himber. The musicians arranged to pull a gag on Richard, in cahoots with the producer and director, that they later regretted for it had almost dire consequences.

While Richard was resting in his dressing room after a rehearsal, the studio clocks were set a half-hour ahead.

As the clocks ticked toward the phony broadcast time, the men climbed on the stand. The on-air light flashed and Richard gave the downbeat on the program's theme. The musicians went into a frenzy of cacophony, each man wailing whatever came into his head.

Himber almost dropped dead. He was so out of it physically and mentally that a substitute conductor had to handle the later broadcast.

CHAPTER 30

Marital Problems

Big-name bandleaders almost always had marital problems, if they were married—and most were—at various times.

They had double-trouble, however, compared with the average husband. Whereas the latter may have spent long hours at a desk, tempted occasionally by a willing secretary, he eventually made it home every day, too tired perhaps for a roll in the sack, but at least he was home.

A name bandleader of the 30's and 40's earned the major portion of his income on the road, a "road" that stretched from Maine to California. Therefore, a popular leader didn't reach the fireside too often, even supposing he had a permanent home base.

Plus which few orchestra wives dug the weary hours and the travails of the open highway.

Which set up inner conflict for both genders.

It's no big secret that women of all ages chase celebrities. And in the Big Band Era, bandleaders and even their musicians were celebrities. More so in the very small towns that housed major ballrooms in virtually every state in the east, midwest, and far west.

As a rule, big band leaders prohibited girls of any age on the bus, even for short runs from one town to another. They also had bans against individual musicians riding with women in private cars (to be sure they showed for the next job).

Consequently, top bands frequently had a comet's tail of cars following the bus from one town to another. Which was dangerous. Especially at night. In Iowa, for example, where a great many major ballrooms existed, the state's two-lane highways (before modern expressways) followed "section-lines," i.e., were built between sections of land. In short, the bus could be bowling along at night at 60 to 70 miles an hour and suddenly be faced with a 90-degree left turn, run a half mile or so, then hit another 90-degree turn-right.

With a professional bus driver those turns were no problem, but too often the women barreling along behind wound up in a corn field. As a matter of fact, many farmers did not erect fences at those corners and did not plant the area. It was a waste of time because so many drivers missed the turns at night despite the road warnings.

Granted sex was not as loose then as it is in the 90's, there nevertheless were eager beavers in every nook and cranny who'd go to bed with a snake if his name was Sammy Kaye, Tommy Dorsey, etc.

There's an old wheeze among males who like to soothe a conscience. It says, "What you don't get at home isn't cheating." Out there were legions of women, old and young, in small towns who wouldn't dare nibble on a husband's jock, but who would give "head" voraciously to a passing name bandleader.

And there were no residual worries. The jock left town the next day, as a rule.

So, the marital existence of a name bandleader was delicately balanced, not only due to the temptations ever confronting the husbands, but also the effect of his often long absences on the female half, who too had feelings and was often tempted.

Bandleaders of note didn't marry "dogs." They could not afford to be seen with anything less than glamorous beauty. So, the wives more often than not were extremely attractive beauties with all the desires of a healthy body. They were "hit on," too, if they stayed home.

Still, few of the wives dared the road. It was too uncomfortable, often grim, for the female. There were no motels as we know them today. Too often, a "motel" meant a group of individual "huts" with no bath, just a "water closet" for relief. Packing and unpacking was a heavy chore and it was difficult to keep clothes in any sort of decent condition.

There were other problems if a wife loved her husband enough to dare the hardships and inconveniences. Dozens of ballrooms were remote from town and no matter how enamored they might have been of the leader they were married to, it was very difficult to sit night after night and listen to the band. There were movie theaters in some small towns, but after a time one saw every film available. Television was still in the future.

In short, what seemed glamorous to the outside world was from the inside a grind that wore everyone to a nub. But, "that's where the money was."

So, there were not many wives who made their husband's bands their life's work, so to speak. Johnny Long was a step below the top grade, but his wife was always with him. Gladys Hampton, as we already pointed out here, wouldn't dare miss collecting Lionel's monies. Vaughn Monroe's wife, Marion, a really great lady, spent a great deal of time on the road, too, but she was a working wife, handling a number of chores.

One wife I never met gave me a ton of laughs. She was married to Lee Castle, a fine trumpeter who led Jimmy Dorsey's band after Jim's death. I liked Lee and we got friendly to the point where, if he wasn't working, he'd occasionally accompany me to the various spots around New York. He lived on the West Side in the 70's. I'd drive up to pick him up and he'd be standing in the lobby. When he saw me he'd slide out of the building and hug the facade for at least 100 yards. I'd pace him. Then he'd run and jump in and off we'd go. He simply didn't want his wife seeing him get into a car. He never explained further.

One wife I know of who had it all was married to a very successful leader. No matter where the band was she knew Ol' Dad had to be on the bandstand at least four hours every evening. And she filled those four hours to the hilt.

Being a nympho of sorts, she had amenable boyfriends all over the place. If the band was in a major city on location, she had companions available at beck-and-call.

On the road, after several trips around the circuit, she had built up a list of phone numbers which served her needs in every town the band might be booked.

And the effort was so pleasant, she didn't mind the road at all.

CHAPTER 31

Manie Sachs

Jack Benny stepped into the limousine and it pulled away, leaving Manie Sachs, President of Columbia Records and a V.P. of Columbia Broadcasting, staring dumfoundedly at a $20 bill Benny had slipped into his hand.

The twenty was a "tip."

The long-term impact of the $20 Benny laid on Sachs that day would not be believed, even by a Hollywood script writer. It projected him from a top recording executive position, albeit "one of the boys," into an "untouchable" as assistant to the great David Sarnoff, founding father of the National Broadcasting Company.

The Bennys had just returned from a European vacation. On their previous trip they had been nailed by customs people trying to smuggle a gaggle of diamonds without paying duty. The ice was confiscated and Benny heavily fined.

This time around, the comedian went through customs like a dose of salts, courtesy of Sachs and a man named Benny. Hence the tip.

CBS had been for some time trying to lure Benny and his top-rated radio program away from NBC, where it was a fixture. CBS offered contracts designed to ease tax burdens on wartime income and had already corralled some of NBC's biggest stars, among them Amos 'n' Andy.

Benny refused all CBS blandishments. He wouldn't even take calls from William Paley, that net's top honcho, who had tried to contact Benny overseas.

In keeping such close tabs on the Bennys' whereabouts, Paley knew when they were due to arrive in New York. He was aware of the fiasco at the end of Benny's previous trip and decided to try easing Benny's entrance into the country as a possible sop. Apparently, he'd heard of the wonders Sachs could do and had done for many, many music biz people. He requested that Manie meet Benny at the Hudson River pier and do what he could to smooth the comedian's re-entry.

Sachs had a "secret weapon" in the form of a music man named Benny Bloom, who could move mountains. For example, *Variety* once sent me on a trip to Hollywood for "seasoning." With wartime restrictions applying, the best the paper could get with all its clout was an upper berth, changing at Chicago. I ran into Bloom at a band opening the night before leaving. After a short phone conversation, Bloom instructed me to go to a certain travel agency the next morning.

Only a few hours before I was to climb into an upper, I picked up a Roomette ticket on a "through" car on the Twentieth-Century Limited to Chicago and the Santa Fe's Chief to Los Angeles.

In short, Bloom was a valuable man to have around. And Manie used him often, paying him off by recording songs owned by Bloom's publishing house.

It would have been understandable if the customs people had run the Bennys through a fine-tooth comb the second time around. Instead, the comedian and his wife were off the ship and in the limo in a half-hour. And Manie, in some ways a bit self-effacing, apparently failed to impress upon Benny his high CBS standing. Benny thought him an "errand boy." So, as he was climbing into the limo, he handed Manie the $20, closed the door, and ordered the chauffeur to take off.

Manie was mortified. He had to tell someone. He chose me, of all people, adding that if I told anyone he'd cut me a new ass. I could not fathom why he told me about it since it was a tremendously embarrassing experience for a man in his position. I can only conclude that he felt if he told me instead of my possibly hearing it from someone else, I would not dare to print anything.

I didn't. Abel, my boss, did. When I'd gotten back to the office that evening, I'd told Green the story. We both howled. But Abel had not promised Manie anything. I did. And Abel crossed me, feeling the item was too good to languish unprinted.

Variety ran down Manie's tribulations in a front-page box the following issue.

When Benny, by then home in Hollywood, read the item, he was mortified at having treated a top CBS exec in that fashion. He phoned Manie. He insisted that the next time Sachs was in Hollywood he must be a Benny house guest. Manie, who never let any grass grow where he walked, arranged a West Coast trip a month later. He and Benny became chums.

In New York a couple months later Manie attended a CBS Board meeting. He heard Paley complaining that Benny still won't answer the phone to him. Enter the hero: Manie picked up the Board Room phone and gave the operator Benny's private number, which rings only at his bedside and which only he answers. In two minutes Benny is on the phone and Manie hands the instrument to Paley, first, of course, advising Benny.

Manie was on the next plane to Hollywood and worked out the basis of a deal that brought Benny to CBS.

Prior to all this NBC had tried to lure Manie from Columbia Records to the post of Artists & Repertoire (A & R) head of RCA-Victor, the NBC subsidiary and, at that time, the largest recording company in the world. Manie had considered a move, but eventually rejected NBC's offer. If Manie moved, it was not going to be into another A & R position.

In the years Manie was at Columbia, he'd always had trouble, however, with Ted Wallerstein and Paul Southard. Together, they had long operated the company. Then Manie was moved in over their heads. They tried their damnedest to shoot him down, primarily because Manie was not a recording man per se. He didn't know shit from chocolate in a control room. He was put in charge to resuscitate the label. His purpose, due to his wide popularity among artists and publishers, was to acquire for Columbia the best and latest songs to record and to corral the best-selling artists to perform them.

And he was backed by Ike Levy, owner of WCAU, Philadelphia, one of the original CBS stockholders and a long-time family friend. It was Ike who powered Manie into the position.

Manie was strong among music people. Public relations was his bag. He'd do such things as run a bus-load of invitees to his Green Valley Country Club outside Philadelphia for a round of golf, lunch there, then transport everyone to the C.& R. Club for dinner, then to old Shibe Park for the Ike Williams—Beau Jack fight. That was one year.

Manie was a power in Philadelphia. My wife and I and Herb Hendler spent a weekend in Philly one year, primarily to see a New York Giants-Philly Eagles football game. As we were leaving the hotel and looking for a cab, a big, black limo screeched to a stop in front of us and Manie popped out. We rode to the game with Manie and the Mayor of Philadelphia.

That was one Manie Sachs. The other side of the coin was a vicious enemy who would wait forever to waylay and bring down anyone whom he felt had knifed him at any past point. I eventually ran afoul of that side of his personality through no fault of my own.

Originally a promotion man for WCAU, where he linked with Levy, Manie later joined MCA in New York. He lived with fellow agent Lou Mindling, who later became a personal manager. He handled Buddy Clark, Dorothy Shay, Martha Tilton (original Benny Goodman vocalist) and others. During the war Mindling came to Manie. Clark was in the service and his family was in financial trouble. To help, Manie gave Clark a one-album record deal, paying him only scale and no royalty for the recordings. Out of it came "Laura," a huge hit. Manie was a hero.

Mindling then offered night club singer Dorothy Shay, "The Park Avenue Hillbilly," a most unlikely candidate as a recording star, a one-album deal, no royalties. Out of that came a smash hit titled "Feudin', Fightin' and Fussin.'"

Again Sachs is a hero.

Naturally, Manie wanted to do it again. He offered Mindling term contracts, with royalty provisions, on both singers. Mindling, figuring he had Manie over a barrel since both singers were coming off hits and figured to have a buying audience in waiting, demurred. He insisted that Columbia pay retroactive royalties on the first albums by each singer before he'd agree to new contracts.

Mindling knew his two artists had gained "booking stature," to coin a phrase, as a result of the hits that Sachs had provided but, he wailed, they hadn't made any money beyond the flat sum they'd been paid for the recording. He was determined to rectify that—besides which, he'd draw a nice cut.

Manie quietly sent an emissary to see Shay to outline the problem. She signed a prepared contract without Mindling's knowledge. He did the same thing with Clark. Both artists separated from Mindling and Manie proceeded to do everything he could to run Mindling out of the business. The next time I heard of Lou he was an agent with William Morris in Chicago.

In the late 40's, The Charlie Spivak Orchestra was nearing the end of a term contract with Columbia. But, he had recorded an unusual version of "White Christmas" and when it was released it began to build into a smash hit. Before it was released, however, Spivak had signed a contract with RCA-Victor to become effective in February when his Columbia deal ended.

Manie accidentally became privy to Spivak's defection. Enraged, he ordered Columbia-distributor promotion men to dissuade disk jockeys from playing the record. He sent distributor salesmen into record stores to actually pull all copies, boxed or unboxed.

The recording died a quick death.

Spivak never came up with another hit, to my knowledge.

Manie was sailing along smartly, a power at CBS because of the Jack Benny deal and a power in the music business because he was a hell of a personal promoter.

Until one day I received a phone call from John Hammond, a good friend since my earliest days on *Variety*, which almost coincided with his joining Columbia. As is well-known, John Hammond, who died in 1989, was a world-renowned jazz aficionado, finder and developer of talent, and a gentleman without parallel in a cut-throat business.

As soon as he heard my voice, John burst out, "Bernie, Manie's out. Wallerstein and Southard finally got him." I didn't believe it since I had been on an extension phone when Ike Levy told Manie to stay where he was when RCA wanted him. I also knew of all the other ways Manie proved valuable to CBS, such as the Jack Benny deal. I expressed doubt.

Hammond said, "How many times have I given you a bum steer?" I could not think of any. "Then take it from there—Manie is history at Columbia," he said.

I dialed Columbia. Ann Fox, switchboard operator, told me Manie had just left for lunch. I hung up and raced up to Lindy's. Manie was there with a couple of publishers. I got him aside, told him of Hammond's statement. When he finished digesting what I said, his only comeback was, "I'll call you later."

I didn't hear from Sachs until Sunday. He called me at home and told me to meet him Tuesday noon on the 52nd floor of the RCA Building. I had a suspicion. The 52d floor was RCA top-level territory. I didn't crack to Abel.

On Tuesday Manie introduced me to General David Sarnoff and advised me he was joining NBC as executive assistant to Sarnoff with offices on the 52d level.

What Manie had done when I tipped him to Columbia's plans to fire him was to reopen the negotiations NBC had launched a few years before, when they had offered him the A & R job at RCA-Victor.

But, he was in a much better position this time than last because of his involvement in the Jack Benny steal. NBC knew by then how the theft of Benny had been accomplished. And that served Manie's purposes. Instead of an A & R job at RCA-Victor he leaped into a top-level slot in the parent company. It only took him three days to land the job after hearing Hammond's disclosure from me.

I never determined why Manie turned on me. There were numerous occasions when he was mad as hell at something I'd written, but it always blew over. He recognized I had a job to do. I suspect, however, that the primary cause was when Manie managed to steal Dinah Shore from RCA-Victor. He deliberately withheld the news until a Monday evening, to benefit me (*Variety* went to press Tuesday). He set up a 6 p.m. meeting attended by Wallerstein and Southard and Joe Higgins, another CRC exec.

When the story hit the paper, Abel, without my knowledge, had edited into the proof a line to the effect that it was no big deal because Dinah's record sales were at a low ebb.

That punctured Manie's triumph. He accepted my explanation, but apparently didn't forget.

After Sachs moved over to NBC, I was handling a singer named Frankie Lester, a feisty 5'4" Italian kid who sang like Sinatra. I'd sold him to RCA's junior "Label X" and he'd recorded a song published by Bobby Mellin, a major name in the biz. The record began to hit, but Bobby couldn't wait for it to build. He went to Joe Carlton, then A & R head of RCA-Victor, and paid him $5,000 to obtain an Eddie Fisher version. Fisher, of course, was then top sales gun on Victor and happened to be coming up for a recording date.

The Fisher version, instead of ballooning the song, killed it off. It was badly arranged and Fisher's vocal was for the birds.

Lester's cut went down the drain, too, because Fisher's side was such a miserable job it destroyed the song.

Before Fisher's recording was released, I racked my brains trying to think of a way to prevent his cut from crowding out Lester's. One night I sat straight up in bed. I had the answer. Next day I went to *Billboard*, the sheet at that point far outdistancing *Variety* as a recording biz chronicle, and sketched an ad, asking whether they would accept it.

The ad said, "Thank you, Eddie Fisher (in small type) for recording (in large letters) Frankie Lester's smash hit - - -."

My objective was to appeal to the nation's disk jockeys to continue playing Frankie's version of the song. For years top name artists had been purloining burgeoning hits by lesser knowns and I knew the jockeys didn't always feel it was right. So, I hoped the ad would persuade them to continue playing Lester as well as Fisher's record.

Fisher was so angry at the audacity of a pip-squeak like Lester coming up with such an ad that his entourage planned an answering ad for the next issue of *Billboard*, one designed to denigrate Lester. He was dissuaded by cooler heads.

However, both Fisher and his manager screamed to high levels at RCA and Sachs got into the squabble. He recognized my handiwork and came after me.

Some time after that when rock began to rear its ugly head, I decided to shuck the management business. Casting around for a new groove in which to use my wide experience, I one day gave Manie a call. He gladly gave me an appointment.

I was ushered into one of the biggest offices I've ever seen. I explained to Manie I'd given up management, mainly because I didn't use marijuana and/or cocaine and didn't know any suppliers. Hence my value to the artists occupying places in the new scheme of things was nil.

Then I found how long he'd been "waiting" for me: Softly, he said with a smile, "I don't hire people, I suggest you see NBC personnel."

"Any particular person?" I asked.

"I have no idea," he answered.

And the chair he was sitting in was one I'd helped him achieve, simply by tipping him off as to what Columbia was planning for him.

Manie died of leukemia in 1957 at only 52. A very untimely and unfortunate closeout of a most unforgettable character.

Agents

No performer in show business —be he or she singer, soloist, actor, or leader of a band—ever succeeded without the aid and advice of the "talent" behind the scene, especially coaches and managers. But the ultimate support was provided by booking agents, men and women who provide the bookings that keep performers afloat financially.

The Big Band Era produced a goodly number of talented agents, most of them solid business men, who often provided financial support and organized careers—who promoted and sold what they conceived—and made a lot of money.

There were a few among the many executives whose habits and foibles lightened the load.

When I joined *Variety* as a messenger, MCA, now one of the giant combines of the overall entertainment industry, was based in Chicago. It had just opened a New York branch, where about a dozen salesmen occupied closely placed desks in one huge room, with glassed-in executive offices along the sides.

And the agency concerned itself mostly with sweet bands—Guy Lombardo, Eddy Duchin, Horace Heidt, Hal Kemp, etc.

MCA had been launched in the 20's by Jules Styne, an ophthalmologist who never practiced his trade, and Billy Goodheart, who retired fairly young to an Indiana farm, after having made his poke booking bands.

That was the early 30's. Six or seven years later, headquarters was at 57th and Fifth, New York, considerably larger and tastefully decorated—where it began losing its sweet-band identity. One of the causes was an ex-University of Pennsylvania student and school bandleader named Willard Alexander, plus Benny Goodman. Willard was a strong advocate of Benny and the kind of music the band played, which was contrary to the agency's aims.

Consequently, he was in constant conflict with the sweet-band adherents among his cohorts.

Since he was a forceful, energetic, often abrasive personality Willard could not get along well with other agency executives.

At this point MCA had grown considerably and not all the executives were concerned solely with bands. Those that were, however, were still sweet-band champions.

From Alexander's frequent conversations with me I gathered that Sonny Werblin, who had risen fast within the ranks, was his main antagonist. They seemed to disagree on everything.

Meanwhile, Goodman's band was turning up beaucoup commissions along with Tommy Dorsey, who had split with brother Jimmy and signed his new band to MCA. All of which tested the agency's stance on the style of music it was accustomed to offer. And that helped cause the friction.

Willard became a powerful MCA personality. It was inevitable, therefore, that he would get offers.

The William Morris Agency, then and now a major factor in the booking end of the entertainment industry and at that time MCA's major rival in things not musical, did not have a big band division. Such was the marquee power of a big band name that not to be able to offer one in conjunction with the booking of their strong comic names, or dancers, etc., became a Morris Agency weakness.

So, Morris offered Willard a deal he could not refuse to build a big band department. He signed a contract—while still with MCA, which had no inkling of his plans. And he wanted to keep it that way. He wanted to shock a few of his MCA enemies.

He devised a plan.

One evening he called me at *Variety*. He asked whether I would be at home the following Sunday at 3 P.M. I assured him I would. At the appointed time he called and detailed his new deal with Morris. However, he failed to spell out for me that his main purpose was to have Werblin and other MCA toppers read of his imminent defection in the Music pages of *Variety*.

When I reached the office Monday morning I mentioned to my boss, Abel, what was going on. He apparently did not believe the story and did what an editor should never ever do. He tried to check. He called Werblin. And the cat was out of the bag. To my dismay, as friendly as Willard Alexander and I had been (I was a guest at his apartment on a number of occasions) we never spoke again until several years later.

Willard's long-thought-out plan for revenge on the MCA men was completely ruined. And he blamed me. Rightly so, I suppose. But, even if I had not discussed it with Abel, the latter would have seen the story in proof and probably would have checked then, too.

I, at that point, was still growing in the gathering of important news and Abel, as Managing Editor, who wrote music news before me and knew people involved, apparently felt I was being taken advantage of; so, he checked. I was furious, but I didn't have a leg to stand on in view of my being a recent, untrained so to speak, addition to the staff.

After some years with Morris and, when Big Bands began to cool off as major marquee powers, Willard Alexander split and set up his own booking agency.

My main man among booking agency executives, however, was Tom Rockwell, major owner of General Artists Corporation. At that time GAC was far in front of MCA as the agent of most of the very top bands available. It is my considered opinion that he had it on any other agency topper in the field. But, unlike MCA men such as Sonny Werblin, who really did not concern himself with music people, Tom more or less confined himself to the Big Bands (except for Perry Como). And he was a smooth, cool operator whose word one could always depend on.

Tom was a former recording exec with Brunswick Records, where he worked with the fabulously successful Boswell Sisters, Glen Gray and his Casa Loma Orchestra, etc. and when he established the agency these acts joined him.

Rockwell originally established GAC in partnership with Cork O'Keefe (the firm name then was Rockwell-O'Keefe). But they had split over a number of differences, one of which was Tom's drinking.

Rockwell built GAC into the strongest band-booking agency in the industry. It handled Jimmy Dorsey, Woody Herman, Artie Shaw, Glen Gray, Glenn Miller, and a long string of others. In other entertainment areas it was not the power that MCA and Morris were. Big Bands was its major.

But to get back to Tom's drinking. In the 30's and 40's credit cards were unknown. Before he left the office each evening his secretary gave him $100 in cash ($300 on Friday) to entertain whoever needed entertaining relative to his purposes. If he got bombed, and he often did, and discussed something with you that needed follow-up talk, he'd say, "Meet me in my office at 9:30 in the morning."

And you'd better be there because he would be there, bright-eyed and ready for anything.

Tom spent every winter at his Hollywood office. I once joined him and a group of others for dinner at Lucy's. We got so sloshed playing a question-and-answer machine for drinks I wasn't sure whether I was in Hollywood or New York. When we left at about midnight he wanted a hamburger. We visited every one of a string of franchised stands, all of which he owned. He insisted on my going home with him. We didn't get to his Monrovia estate until 3 a.m.

Rockwell had a fishing cabin on a lake in Canada, equipped with a Chris-Craft cruiser, hardly a fishing boat. When he sold the cabin he had the boat shipped to a Hollywood mooring. The Saturday after its arrival, Tom and Henry Miller, head of the Hollywood office, got sloshed. Tom insisted on going for a boat ride (at midnight). It was foggy.

Wide-open in the Catalina Channel, they ran head-on into a large bell-buoy, which apparently was not doing much "belling."

Miller was pitched overboard. The boat, with its bow smashed almost to the cockpit, went down like a stone. Tom went down with the ship, until he floated free. The two swam to the buoy and spent the rest of the night, drenched and frozen, listening to the bell bong above them because they had disturbed it by climbing aboard. They were rescued in the morning.

That was Tom Rockwell. I played many rounds of golf with him and his second in command, Art Weems, a very popular and capable man whom I liked immensely. As a matter of fact, these two men were the main reason I signed the Ralph Flanagan Orchestra to GAC, when every agency in the business was hot after the band.

One of the rival agency heads who got very angry with me when I signed Flanagan with GAC was Joe Glaser, head of Associated Booking Corp. He was the epitome of show-business characters. I was extremely close to Joe (you must be close with a man who, on the way to a weekly lunch, stops at a bank and shows you more than $100,000 in cash stashed in a vault).

Glaser's handling of himself didn't come close to the outward class and suave approach that characterized most of his rival agents. He was rough and tough with language to match and could use his hands when necessary. But under all that he was a softie. His hobby was raising miniature Boston bulldogs, several of which won AKC ribbons (he had one bedroom in his New York penthouse fitted only with dog cages).

I came across Glaser almost at the time he reached New York from Chicago. His "agency" then was himself and secretary Frances Church.

Joe once told me the story of how he owned the Grand Terrace, a South Chicago club. One winter a.m., he detailed, two hoods he knew walked in and asked him if he had an overcoat. When he agreed he did, he was advised to go get it. They then ushered him into a limo and drove him to the airport and advised him not to return.

Glaser was not a well-schooled man. He dictated letters to Francis that were one long sentence. And he brooked no changes. Commas, periods, paragraphs. What were they? But he knew how to make money. He managed Lionel Hampton, Louis Armstrong, Les Brown, and a long string of others.

When Joe died, in the late 50's, he didn't have a single heir. His ex-wife, he once told me, ran a brothel in Cleveland or Cincinnati.

He left the whole operation to his office boy, whom I knew only as "Oscar."

I have mentioned Cork O'Keefe several times in this tome. A great talent manager, he was the exact opposite of any other executive in the business. I was well acquainted with him while on *Variety*, but became much closer when we rented part of his office space in what was then the RKO Building, next to the Radio City Music Hall, to operate the Ralph Flanagan and Buddy Morrow Orchestras.

Cork was quiet, unassuming. A devout Catholic, he practiced what he didn't preach, contrary to many of the Catholics I've known. But he knew his business and was often the target of people in the business who didn't know theirs.

An agency man I also liked immensely was Russ Lyon, one of the many MCA rank-men. One of the things I remember clearly is his dealing me two pat gin hands after a round of golf at his Plandome, Long Island, golf club. I took him at golf and, very guiltily, at cards.

One fateful day Russ was advised his wife had tuberculosis. Within days he had sold his house, quit MCA, and moved to Phoenix. There he got into real estate, opened his own agency, and went on to millionaire status. In the process, he induced Al

Gazely, who had been Billy Goodheart's executive assistant at MCA before Goodheart retired, to join him in Phoenix. Al worked for Russ and eventually opened his own agency, following Russ into the higher financial regions.

Another great agent was a man named Charlie Yates, involved with Bob Hope in the comic's early days. Yates was an outstanding golfer, playing to a scratch handicap. He's remembered by me as the man who taught me how to hit a golf ball out of a pond— six inches below the surface.

At a relatively young age, Charlie had a most acceptable death—to his way of thinking, I'm certain. He rolled off a moving golf cart and died of a heart attack on the fairway.

One of the most unlikely talent managers, but never an agent, was a man named "Bullets" Durgom, ultimately a big man in Hollywood circles. From New Jersey, Durgom began his career by hanging around Frank Dailey's Meadowbrook. He became band-boy to Tommy Dorsey's Orchestra, a low spot on any totem pole. In the process, however, he managed to sign personal management contracts with almost every one of T.D.'s singers, with the exception of Frank Sinatra. He had contracts with Jo Stafford, Dick Haymes, the Pied Pipers, etc., all of which he sold off for nice pieces of change when they became stars.

Durgom, gnome-like in appearance, but personality-plus, also achieved a contract with Jackie Gleason, when Gleason was a relative nonentity. Before Jackie began to build into a star, Durgom hied himself to Hollywood, where he developed important contacts and friendships and began doing very well.

Meanwhile, Jackie, a not very high-priced night-club comic, had reached into TV via the Dumont network and was on the launching pad of a fabulous career. He bugged Durgom to return east and help. Durgom wanted Hollywood, not Gleason.

In Hollywood at the time was Jack Philbin, who had been a song plugger, an agency executive, husband to Marion Hutton, Glenn Miller's singer, and was now managing Ina Ray Hutton's (no relation) fading all-girl Orchestra.

Durgom deputized Philbin, at $400 weekly, to go east and handle Gleason's affairs, as a means of getting Gleason off his back. Gleason was not too happy with the move—but became very happy with Philbin. When Durgom's contract ran out, Philbin became Gleason's manager. And Philbin had found his groove.

A very astute operator, Jack did a great job with Gleason. When Gleason took a European vacation one summer in the early 50's, he turned the TV time period over to Philbin, and Jack created a high-rated summer "vaudeville" show, backed by the re-formed Dorsey Brothers Orchestra, which gave Elvis Presley his first TV network exposure.

Then there was (and very likely still is) the kind of manager who turns sour after success. One of the greatest of singers—Nat King Cole—had that sort of problem. Occupying a level far above most rivals, Nat came crashing to earth when one day the IRS sought to attach everything he owned—house, cars, clothing. They wanted everything.

It turned out that, although his manager Carlos Gastel had had income returns properly prepared, the monies due had not been forwarded. Nat was unaware of the default. He was in deep trouble.

My accountant, Phil Braunstein, who was also the financial mentor of Tommy Dorsey and a long list of show-business people, was drawn into the picture. Well-known and highly respected by the IRS, he extricated Nat by working out a deal under which the unpaid taxes were paid without such heavy penalties as forfeiture of everything Nat had worked for over the years.

A personal manager generally is among the most maligned characters in show business. One of the reasons for the bad attitude toward them lies in the many fast-tongued phonies who can and frequently do talk unsuspecting tyro talent into contracts and then do nothing but harm, if they do anything at all.

Then,if the performer makes strides via his own effort or pure dumb luck, the phony is all too willing to settle the contract for a sum.

This kind of leech is often matched by the performers who, after a manager's astuteness creates them and steers their talent to success, firmly believe it all was accomplished by no one but themselves. Such ego would not allow the belief of any other reason for success.

CHAPTER 33

Press Agents

Show business could not survive without its promotion men—the people who keep things hopping and without whom the "entertainment" section of any newspaper in the country wouldn't be worth reading.

There were great ones during the Big Band Era and there were phonies—hangers-on who didn't know their business and who'd literally beg for a morsel of type about a client.

But one of the best was a man named Kay Hansen.

"Mr. Woods, there's a Colonel Hansen here to see you."

I couldn't believe my secretary's statement. This was 1951. I had not seen Kay Hansen since 1943 and hadn't heard from him since 1945 or thereabouts. And here he was—a Colonel yet.

Kay was one of the best press agents ever to blow media horns for the top bandleaders of the time, among them Artie Shaw's "Begin the Beguine" Orchestra.

219

Down under, Kay was also a deep patriot, which I had not noticed despite many hours of tennis and badminton, card games, family dinners, etc. I also didn't know that he was a Reservist in the U.S. Army. And soon after Pearl Harbor, Kay applied for a Commission. Already 43 years old, he was rejected. But the age limit for enlisting in the regular Army was raised in 1943 to 45 years, Kay quickly became a buck private. He left a wife (Gertrude) and a business partner. The next I heard was a post-card from Fort Hood, Texas.

After hugs and handshakes in my office, I suggested lunch at Lindy's. Exiting the building, I whistled for a cab, but before one could reach us a chauffeured Army car parked in front of the Radio City Music Hall pulled up and Kay ushered me into it. I flipped.

During lunch, I got the lowdown. Via breaks, hustle, and his press-agent's knowhow, Kay had risen quickly through the ranks and was at that moment and had been for most of the last part of the war an aide to General Omar Bradley.

A few years later I read that Kay died of a heart attack in Paris, where he had accompanied Bradley to a peace conference.

Then I saw the film "Patton." In it Bradley's involvement with Patton is somewhat detailed and the name "Hansen" comes up repeatedly during the runoff.

As anyone in show business knows, promotion and publicity are the name of the game. Press agents often move mountains. And there is no question that on many an occasion their work is the difference between box-office success and drainsville. Of course, their efforts to make something out of anything is always subject to the public's acceptance of what's being promoted. Any good promotion man knows you can promote the public only so far. If the talent or show or film doesn't have it, there isn't enough media attention in the world to make it work for any length of time.

One of the best Broadway promotion men I ever came across was George Lottman. My first meeting with him and an assistant was amusing in light of later years. As I've said elsewhere, when Abel Green told me to "go, be a reporter" I left the office and walked to 46th and Broadway, stood there and reflected on what to do next. I did not have the slightest idea where to start. But I recalled a promotion piece we received the previous day outlining a new entertainment room that the Astor Hotel, on Times Square, was building.

Lottman's office was in the Astor. I went in and for the first time used the phrase "Bernie Woods—of *Variety*, to see Mr. Lottman." Believe me, my voice was not near as confident as that looks in print. The receptionist asked me to wait.

I waited fifteen minutes. A young fellow came out and introduced himself to me as Howard Richmond, Lottman's assistant. We talked. He gave me a tour of the construction mess of the new room. Then I met Lottman.

Years later, after Howie Richmond had become an important music publisher, as was his father, we talked about that day. Then he told me that it had been his first day on the job. When my name was announced, he had scooted into the men's room to comb his hair and straighten his tie before coming out to meet the "big *Variety* reporter."

George Evans was another great press agent whom I came across in the earliest days of reporting. He was already connected with Glenn Miller and was promoting the band's "Sunrise Serenade" recording on Decca. George and his assistants were tremendously creative. I have long heard the story that, while working for Benny Goodman, they devised the idea of getting kids to dance in the aisles during Benny's first performance at the Paramount Theater, New York, a stunt that made every newspaper and magazine in the country.

David O. Alber was another press agent I met in my very early days. He was also at that time not long in the business. He handled Sammy Kaye and a number of radio personalities and provided me with enough one-or two-paragraph blurbs to at least have a few things in every *Variety* edition.

Jack Egan was Tommy Dorsey's man. I don't believe he ever handled any other personality. A crackerjack at his work and an outstanding personality, Tommy heavily relied on his knowhow.

There are a number of nationally known newspaper columnists, past and present, who would be more familiar with a shovel and a ditch if it weren't for the press agents.

CHAPTER 34

Andy Griffith

A newspaperman as a rule has many friends. Some are genuine and some are there because of his access to the printed page.

I was no different. I had loads of pals. Often it was difficult to weed out the ones seeking a ride, for one reason or another.

Dick Linke was one of my real friends. He was a sharp, independent promotion man with his own office, handling Sammy Kaye's Orchestra, among other acts.

Dick and his wife Margaret and Lorraine and I would frequently visit each other's homes or dine together.

As I did with Herb Hendler I often discussed going into business with Dick. We'd get into it often without ever doing anything about it.

Then without much warning Dick folded his office and joined Capitol Records' New York office as head of its promotion department. He had gotten tired of generating his own income and wanted to get out from under office rent and secretary-salary obligations.

A little later, Herb Hendler and I made the decision to partner in the management of the Ralph Flanagan Orchestra. Dick's nose was out of joint, but he never said a word.

One weekend after the explosive debut of Flanagan at Meadowbrook, Lorraine and I planned a party at our Bayside, New York, home. Dick and Margaret were to come, but on the prior Thursday, Margaret phoned and said they couldn't make it. Dick was being sent out of town by Capitol. The company's Hollywood execs had asked him to fly to North Carolina and check out a supposed hit recording by a local artist.

Usually the company's Artists and Repertoire executives were responsible for such things, but none were available (they probably invented reasons to duck the trip). So Dick, hardly in a position to refuse, drew the assignment.

In those days small, local recording companies in various parts of the country—but particularly in the southeast, which was "country" territory—often tried to falsify sales figures of a local hit recording, hoping to steal a high price for it's sale to one of the majors. And Capitol apparently distrusted this one. They wanted everything checked out.

It turned out to be the task of a lifetime.

When Linke returned on Monday he called me at my office and said he'd bought the recording for Capitol. In addition, he explained, "I signed the guy to a personal management contract." He was gleeful about finally making the move he'd always wanted.

The song was titled "What It Was Was Football."

The name of the artist: Andy Griffith.

One of the first things Linke did with Griffith was get him a part in the upcoming Broadway production of *No Time for Sergeants*. Then on to Hollywood for the film version.

The rest is history. Dick for some time was a major power in Hollywood TV circles, with contracts on Don Knotts and Jim Nabors, among others. He was widely known among Sunset Boulevard management and production circles for his two-telephone limousine.

All that occurred in the middle 50's and Dick Linke and Andy Griffith were together for years. Both their marriages sank, however.

CHAPTER 35

Music Business

The Big Bands and the beautiful music they played, which many music writers misname as "jazz," held the public ear for no more than twelve to fifteen years, give or take a few opinions, while rock music has been riding high for more than thirty years.

Why has rock so far surpassed the great music written then and played so superbly by the Big Bands? That's almost impossible to define. So much of rock is raw and uncouth in relation to the musical sounds made during the time of the Big Bands. One can hardly call the difference musical progress.

The music biz of the 30's and 40's was a money-making proposition, as is rock today, but most song writers then had a personal mission to turn out the best constructed material possible. Modern writers seem to write for expediency—they have a recording date coming up. Write! Fill a void. Even one-word "lyrics" often do.

It is difficult for anyone bred into and accustomed to musical material that made sense, to listen to modern material. Anyone from that era must feel that while everything else in this world progresses and improves, popular music generally has steadily gone downhill.

The music of the 30's and 40's and that of the 70's, 80's and 90's are poles apart from every conceivable aspect—including the pockets into which the ultimate earnings pour.

However, there is no comparing the financial aspect of the two systems. The income to the modern music industry dwarfs that of the Big Band era in every conceivable way. The initial sale of a smash Glenn Miller recording, for example, did well to surpass one million copies. That's chickenfeed compared with any current giant rock hit, which can total ten to twenty times that number.

The Benny Goodman or the Tommy Dorsey bands of the early 40's seldom. if ever, reached one million dollars in earnings in one year. Glenn Miller went over that figure most of his brief years while at the top of the heap mainly due to his five-nights-a-week Chesterfield radio broadcasts.

In contrast, a smash rock group of the 90's can pick up a million or so on one date in a modern ball park. However, that same major rock group can play what was called a "one-nighter" in the Big Band days, only once a week or so, if that often. The huge task of setting up giant sound systems, which are the absolute primary requirement of any rock performance anywhere (the decibels are part of the studied impact), plus the lighting and all else required to give the followers of the "grail rock" what they pay highly to hear, takes days to set up and tear down and requires a large crew and a caravan of vehicles. All very expensive.

I recall an amusing story I once wrote for *Variety* that perhaps epitomizes the difference between the operations of the two eras and the financial results. It involved Guy Lombardo's Orchestra, one of the most successful of the "sweet" bands of the 30's and 40's. Guy didn't often play one-nighters in the big ballrooms of the country mainly because his musical style didn't always fit the neighborhood, but such was the discipline in his band that when it finished a ballroom date each musician was responsible for packing and stowing aboard the band's bus his own instrument, music, uniform, etc. In this way, Lombardo's bus was rolling down the exit driveway within fifteen minutes after "Auld Lang Syne."

But, all Lombardo took with him as a result of the night's work seldom was more than $3,500.

The Big Band years comprised an overall music industry as different from these rock years as the vast difference in cash income to the two eras. From the writing of a song, who wrote it, the recording, the promotion, and the distribution of profits, it was a different ball game. A number of organizations were involved, each profiting from a hit according to the way each contributed.

Today, the profits more often bulge the pockets of a single artist or group.

Songwriting was a separate profession in the early days and into the Big Band Era (musicians seldom wrote songs; neither did leaders, although some had their names applied to new material as a sop or a bribe). Some writers worked alone. Many worked in pairs. Some were trained musically. Others were not. Professional writers, and I emphasize professional, such as Richard Rodgers, Oscar Hammerstein, Lorenz Hart, Jerome Kern, were at their best when they sat down to write a tune to fit a specific scene in a Broadway musical or a Hollywood film. But out of their efforts to design a song to further a plot, came some of the greatest songs ever written— tunes that also became huge pop hits—tunes that will be played and sung years from now, despite the overwhelming flood of rock.

That calibre of writer didn't often draw ideas out of the blue. When and if they did, the song likely was stashed until a production spot was found to fit. The story goes, for example, that Rodgers got the idea for "My Heart Stood Still" when a companion ejaculated that phrase in a Paris cab as its driver barely eluded a crash. Oscar Hammerstein's great tune "There's a Small Hotel" was written about a country hostelry with fine food in Stockton, New Jersey, near his Pennsylvania farm.

And they did not write one-word "lyrics" or lyrics that had little meaning, inserted only because something was needed to fit a beat or to fill out a recording date. Of course, the 40's music men came up with crazy tunes occasionally, like "Mairzy Doats," but they were understandable and most had some, albeit weird, meaning.

Below the level of the Hammersteins and others, however, the 40's spawned dozens of excellent craftsmen. Writers such as Jimmy Van Heusen, Johnny Burke, and Johnny Mercer, wrote for Hollywood productions as well as "free lance," so to speak. And below that level were hundreds of accomplished "hacks" with no connections who went from publisher-to-publisher demonstrating their wares. Others had agreements that gave one publisher first choice, which didn't necessarily guarantee a publisher's acceptance of new material.

Every songwriter of any note wound up with a trunkful of rejects that didn't make a dent when written, but found acceptance years later. "See You In September" was such an item.

After a 30's or 40's new song was placed with a publisher, the latter then had to "sell" the tune to a record company executive to achieve a recording. In the days of which we speak, performers didn't own their own labels (or companies). There were only four recording companies—RCA-Victor, Columbia, Decca and later Capitol, which meant strong competition for every available record-date opening. That led to other niceties such as bribes of all kinds, from cash to sex. But no drugs.

If a song was recorded, the publisher planned its promotion. The more important the recording artist the heavier the push by the plugger staff to make a hit. If a lesser artist was involved, it might be relegated to what music men called our "No. 2" or "No. 3" plug, which meant a somewhat weaker effort.

If a "headliner" had cut the tune, often little effort was necessary to make it a hit. That was the millennium.

Major publishers had staffs of "song pluggers" whose job it was to achieve broadcast performances of new songs in any way possible so as to make the general public aware. (In the remote "old days" song pluggers had to be reasonably good singers and pianists. They would even go into Woolworth stores with pianos and sing and/or play new songs while patrons shopped.)

But, during the Big Band Era of the music industry, before disk jockeys became equally powerful plugs, the main avenues of promotion were the Big Bands. Every night in the week the radio stations in every city and hamlet across the country (TV was unknown) carried band "remotes." Most stations were aligned with either NBC's Blue or Red Network (the Red later became ABC), CBS, or the Mutual Network. The air time consisted of unsponsored, usually half-hour pickups from dozens of major hotels and cafes in New York, Boston, Chicago, Los Angeles, San Francisco, etc. Each network would carry four bands a night, from 11 P.M. to 1 A.M. closing. No commercial sponsors were interested in time that late, so it was clear air.

That system afforded a tremendous amount of promotion time for all involved. It (1) made the public aware of the names of the bandleaders and (2) promoted songs. The air time also highlighted the "clubs." Such frequent origination points as Frank Dailey's Meadowbrook, Cedar Grove, New Jersey, the Cafe Rouge of the Pennsylvania Hotel, New York, the Sherman and Edgewater Beach Hotels, Chicago, and the Palladium Ballroom, Hollywood, among others, were almost household words, particularly Dailey's Meadowbrook, which originated as high as 24 broadcasts a week.

The networks also frequently found themselves with unsponsored air during the day. WOR ran into that minor crisis one summer and again I was provided with an unusually funny story for *Variety*. The period involved was in the middle of the afternoon. Tommy Tucker's band was working a spot called Murray's, Tuckahoe, New York, which had a huge swimming pool. Naturally, Tucker's men didn't stray far in the summer heat. Joe Galkin, Tucker's manager, advised WOR his band was always available if free time came up. At a moment's notice the musicians could be on the stand ready to go. And it worked beautifully. Tucker got a lot of valuable air time.

As Galkin was telling me about the arrangement during a round of golf I got the mental picture of WOR hitting an alarm bell and the musicians sliding down a brass pole onto the bandstand while Tucker raised his arm for the downbeat. It came out a hell of a hilarious item for *Variety*.

However, there was a downside to all this: The availability of air time and the value of it to a band's progress induced leaders to accept major hotel and club bookings at a weekly financial loss. Depending on the caliber of the band, its size, and its prominence (better musicians cost more) that loss could be considerable. But the deficit was usually made up when, after closing out a hotel or club run of four to six weeks and literally hundreds of self-promoting broadcasts, the band would hit the road on a long string of one-nighters, which brought beaucoup financial return.

After weeks on the road, "dancing" across country, the band would "locate" again at one of the major bookings with a "wire" and begin the process all over again.

The value to the bandleaders of the heavy schedule of nightly broadcasts was matched by the value to music publishers and kept their staffs busy every night "plugging." If their "professional managers," as the top plugger was called, had managed to get a song recorded by a band on location at a hotel or club, then it was a snap to get the leader to schedule the song on virtually every broadcast, for obvious reasons. But if, as more frequently was the case, a band with air time had not recorded a particular song, the task was tough. Enter a plugger's "personality." If he wasn't that friendly with a leader, bribes might or might not follow. But, as I mentioned before, no drugs.

These nightly broadcasts were so important to publishers that to have a song eliminated from one after the bandleader had promised a "plug" often led to conflicts. Woody Herman once "pulled a plug" on a song being promoted by perhaps his closest friend—Juggy Gayles. He did it to help another publisher who was on a "drive" (getting as many plugs as possible in one week). Juggy was with me driving back from the Meadowbrook. We were listening to Woody from the Cafe Rouge of the old Pennsylvania Hotel.

When the air shot was over and Juggy's song was among the missing, Jug screamed, "Pull over" as soon as he saw a roadside phone. He reached Woody, who explained he did it to help another song plugger in dire need, adding, "You're my friend; I figured you'd understand."

Juggy bellowed, "Don't be my friend, play my song," and slammed down the phone. That crack became a Tin Pan Alley rallying cry.

Another publisher who had a song eliminated from a broadcast in a similar fashion got so angry that he slugged the bandleader a few minutes after he went off the air.

To broadcast or play any song a band had to have an arrangement (now called a "chart"). Simply, that's a "part" for each musician to play in conjunction with the other instruments. Arrangements were costly. Too, the "copyist," the guy who extracted each "part" from the master arrangement, was another bill. A band already losing money on "location," couldn't or wouldn't pay for an arrangement just to give a guy a plug, unless the plugger was a close friend (enter the "personality" angle again). Or, if the plugger's firm paid the arranger's tab, which happened often though it was an industry no-no.

That practice, though, usually was confined to bands less successful. The top names wouldn't stoop that low.

There were plenty of bands striving to make it to the big money without wherewithal. I clearly recall reviewing Les Brown's Orchestra, brand new and on its first really important booking at the Glen Island Casino, New Rochelle, New York. When I left, Les intercepted me at the door to apologize for not picking up my Coke-sized tab. He explained he was broke.

A good part of a top professional manager's job was to romance record company "Artists & Repertoire" executives, the men who unearthed and signed artists and selected the songs to be recorded. These people, obviously, meant life or death to music industry folk, for in those days a song without a recording was headed for quick oblivion. (Today a song is never published unless it has been recorded). This, of course, set up more bribery problems, which took many forms.

But, no drugs were ever involved. Booze and sex—yes. But again, no drugs.

A hit song produced big profits, then (much more now) and the financial results were split many ways, as a rule. Unless one was a Bing Crosby, the artist drew only five percent of the sale price of each record sold, which at that time ranged from 35 cents to 75 cents. The publishers of the songs on each side of a disk drew two cents each. (The firm owning the tune on the reverse side of a big hit, was in on a pass; it drew the same royalty). The songwriter or writers got their cut from the publisher's end (usually one of the two cents, which they split). Both publisher and songwriter(s) also got a semi-annual cut of the take from the American Society of Authors and Publishers, which licenses users of copyrighted music for profit, for example, night clubs, ballrooms, television networks or independent TV stations, radio stations.

Years ago the heaviest income came from sales of sheet music, a profit form that has virtually vanished.

For a long time the ASCAP split was inequitable in that each writer got the same amount (if there were three or four writers of a song, the same held true). But, if a songwriter wrote both music and lyric alone, the ASCAP payoff to him was the same as any single of a co-written song received.

Because of Irvin Berlin, who always wrote both the music and lyrics, and for years was classed simply as an "A" member on the same level as any writer of either music or lyric, a writer of both lyric and music now receives the credit he or she deserves for writing both ends. ASCAP finally elevated Berlin onto a "Double-Double A" level, thereby putting such writers in a class by themselves.

But modern rock artists don't concern themselves much with distribution of profits. When money is on the line all signals are off. The artist(s) usually consumes the whole pie. Singers and/or bands almost always write their own material, as miserable as a vast amount of it may be; they record it themselves (in company studios), they publish it themselves, don't do much promotion except work with disk jockeys. And they pocket it all, including the ASCAP or Broadcast Music, Inc. payoffs, which today are considerable.

New artists come and go—down the drain faster than comets blow across the sky. Frequently, it's one record and never heard of again.

But the ones that hit big and stick around take out millions. They make the earnings of the best-known bandleaders and music publishers of the Big Band Era seem like pocket change.

Unfortunately the quality of music and its purveyors has dropped to miserable levels. The "secondary" singers and performers of years gone by were far more accomplished at their trade than 90 percent of what today is passing for "talent."

Virtually all industries progress, find better methods to the same ends. All the modern music business can claim is that it has gotten louder without improving substance. When the decibels are cut, the music industry is a whisper of its former self.

CHAPTER 36

Disk Jockeys

It's long forgotten by now, but there was a time when the music industry took an extremely dim view of disk jockeys, a form of radio broadcasting that is today the main reason for many AM and FM outlets to be on the air.

In the mid-1920's a Philadelphia radio station, apparently with a great deal of foresight, began broadcasting pop recordings in its daily schedule. A group of New York music publishers, joined by bandleaders, including the Casa Loma Orchestra and Paul Whiteman, felt the idea was a no-no, that the station was providing for nothing a product that provided part of their annual income. They sued.

In delivering his decision, the presiding judge shocked the music people. He said, "A recording purchased from a proper source is no longer the property of the manufacturer or the performer. The buyer may use it in any way he sees fit, including broadcasting its contents."

It did not occur to the suing group that broadcast play of a recording by a band or personality would become free advertising, possibly increasing rather than decreasing the value of the recording and the artist.

They were flabbergasted at what happened as a result. Record sales jumped in Philly and the idea spread fast to other cities and towns.

Ergo, the "Disk Jockey" was born.

Eventually, both the music publishing industry and every bandleader who could afford it, were spending huge sums annually to curry favor with jockeys in major and minor cities from coast to coast.

And every major city had its star "jock," the #1 man who had such a hold on the local listening public that he could make or break the sale of a particular recording simply by playing it repeatedly or not playing it at all.

And how those "stars" worked their roles.

To make it more interesting, some major markets had multiple stars whose listener ratings were not too far apart. That's when the crap really hit the fan for artists and their promotion men. Tiptoeing became a new art to them in trying to avoid offending rival jocks.

Wined, dined, laid, and relaid was the applicable approach. Jocks played it to the hilt.

In Boston, for example, there was Bob Clayton on WHDH, the undisputed power, riding a signal that ranged wide in New England. Close to him was Norm Prescott on WORL. Woe betide any bandleader, singer, or publisher who went to Prescott first with a live interview or a newly released recording. They would become verboten on WHDH.

Prescott eventually wound up as a third or fourth man on WNEW, New York.

Every major station in the country sent representatives to New York occasionally to tape WNEW's operation and stay up with what the big city was doing. And the kingpin of WNEW was Martin Block.

In my considered opinion, Block was the epitome of jocks anywhere. A deep, smooth, easily identifiable voice. Intelligent, convincing commercials, and a thorough knowledge of the music business made Block a standout.

Block had been an assistant to Al Jarvis, a Los Angeles jock who originated the tag, "Make Believe Ballroom." Block applied it to his New York show. After ten years or so in New York, he wanted to move back to Los Angeles. His intention was to do a live show there and tape or record his shows for WNEW a week in advance.

Block bought a minor ranch in Encino, where I visited him soon after the move, in company with Joe Shribman, manager of Rosie Clooney and Tony Pastor. And he told us one of the funniest stories.

Block had moved his wife to California before moving the show. And he was delayed. She was West perhaps six weeks when she sent him a wire saying, "The colored handyman gets whiter every day." No dope, Block immediately scheduled a Friday evening plane trip West. He feared flying. He went to his doctor for something to keep him asleep in flight. The doc prescribed some pills, with certain instructions. Block screwed it up.

When the relatively slow DC-6 landed at LAX he could not function. He was stretchered off the plane and hospitalized. He

wasn't released until Monday, at which point he was forced to go
from the hospital to a plane back to New York.

He howled when he told Joe and me the story and showed us
his wife's wire.

Many of the jocks of the 40's and 50's used screwball
approaches just as many of the moderns sound like they are out
of their minds.

Milwaukee had a nut called "Coffee-Head" Larsen, a morning
jock who did everything he could think of to sexually titillate
housewives. He was so successful it wasn't funny.

During news breaks he'd take calls from lonely, unfulfilled
women. I heard him one A.M. tell a caller, "I'll stick a tongue into
you so far you'll taste it." He'd go into detail in all directions, then
hold the phone so you could hear the screams of delight.

Larsen was far from alone. Frustrated housewives in all parts
of the country get on the phone with jocks and get sex talk going.
With the invention of the seven-second delay, any really x-rated
dialogue can be blocked out before it reaches the airwaves. They
get off the nut with a stranger without leaving the house.

There was a jock in Washington, D.C., whose name I cannot
remember, who devised a contest in which the top prize was dinner with him at any glitzy spot they chose, then on to whatever
they wanted to do. He rounded up a long list of willing females
that he used for a long time.

There was a late-night nut in Boston—Sherm Feller (who I
believe is now the ballpark announcer for the Red Sox). Music
publishers, artists, and managers were always dropping into his
studio since he had a sizable audience. He had a weird fetish.
He'd play the disk you were promoting, make talk and often,
without a word, get up and leave the studio and go downstairs for
coffee, leaving you to carry on the show.

The jocks of the 40's and 50's were a curious mixture. There were quiet, businesslike men like Block, Eddie Gallaher (WTOP, Washington, D.C.), Paul Brenner of WAAT, Newark, New Jersey, Howard Miller of Chicago.

One early morning jock whom I still call if I'm driving through Richmond, Virginia, which my wife and I did often while living In Florida, was Harvey Hudson (WLEE). He graduated from disk jockey to two-term mayor of the city of Richmond, so strong was his impact.

CHAPTER 37

Accidents

It has always been amazing to me how few serious road accidents befell the Big Bands. In order to make it financially, thousands of miles had to be covered every year. And high-speed expressways were nonexistent. The only one then-available was the Pennsylvania Turnpike, a rather narrow and dangerous roadway. When it opened it had no speed limit.

The more prominent the band, the more time it had to spend on the road. That's where the money was—in small-town ball-rooms from Maine to California.

Virtually all travel was by bus or private car with heavy emphasis on the former. It was impossible to consistently operate by rail. Rarely was a sizable ballroom along the tracks.

So, the nation's two-lane highways were the only answer.

A vast majority of the leaders much preferred moving by bus simply because when the bus arrived the entire band was on hand, fairly well relaxed since most musicians learned to rest in the "Iron Lung". Secondly, travel by private car was very risky due to necessary night movement, which heightened the possibility of accidents. And if something did happen to just one of a group of cars and its occupants did not arrive at a booking on time, the entire band might as well have blown it. It's difficult to sound like a cohesive musical combination with three or four sidemen missing.

A method of saving money for the musicians also helped wear them out on long strings of one-nighter bookings. A road manager would set up a trek using "two-fers." This meant getting two sleeps for one in any hotel or motel. It worked on the basis of the check-in and check-out times.

As a rule check-in was after 7 a.m. and check-out varied from noon to three p.m. the following day. Thus a band could ride all night after closing the previous dance, check-in at 7 a.m. or later, sleep all or most of the day, play that night, then come back to the same hotel and sleep again. At 9 or 10 a.m. next morning, depending on how far it was to the next booking, the band would take off for the next date and repeat the process.

Thus, the men would pay for one night's lodging fees for two days' sleep.

The American Federation of Musicians travel rule prohibited any band from traveling more than 400 miles in any 24 hours. But in the 30's and 40's there were so many ballrooms featuring name bands that mileage from one to another often was only 200 miles or so. When that happened, the leaders would see many of the same fans both nights. Driving that distance to dance to their favorite was no problem.

A pair of dates almost finished the Flanagan band—and me with it—late one afternoon in Iowa. The road manager had pegged the takeoff time from where we were to that night's job at 4 p.m., since the next job dance was only 75 miles away, he said. Then came his frantic call to everyone to board the bus. That night's date was more than 150 miles. He had goofed.

We were on a two-lane highway. It made a long, sweeping turn to the left. What couldn't be seen was that the turn ended on a relatively narrow bridge across a river. Then the highway made a long, sweeping turn to the right. As we entered the bridge a huge gasoline tank truck hit the opposite entrance at the same moment. Both vehicles were moving fast.

The encounter was so close that bridge girders folded our right side mirror against the bus and the truck did the same to the left mirror.

I still have a mental picture of what would have happened if that bridge had been even a foot narrower.

In all the time of the Big Bands I know of only a few major accidents. Orville Knapp, a secondary leader, was killed in a light-plane crash in New England. Enoch Light, then a secondary bandleader who spent most of his working time in hotels, had a head-on crash which put him in a hospital bed for a long stretch and out of the band business. (He started a record company while abed.)

The most unusual road stumble I recall involved Vaughn Monroe's Orchestra. Moving by bus along a country road, the bus engine suddenly burst into flame. Since the fire was in the rear, no one noticed. When they did, the men had time only to get out of the vehicle. They lost everything, including instruments, and were stranded in the boondocks.

One of the weirdest accidents I ever heard of involved a singer—Buddy Clark—who did well as a single after having a smash hit record on Columbia titled, "Laura."

I knew Buddy well—knew his brashness and aggressiveness. I once stood with him in front of a Providence hotel, talking with the city's most prominent disk jockey and his fiancee, and listened to Buddy try to talk the girl into coming up to his room. Neither I nor the jock could believe our ears. Buddy was about to be slugged when he laughed it off, saying he was just kidding. He wasn't.

Buddy's brashness eventually killed him in the stupidest way. Living in Hollywood then, he accompanied a friend by car to a football game at Stanford University in Palo Alto, about 300 miles north. Leaving the stadium after the game, he came across four friends who had flown up in a light plane.

Not feeling like the long drive home, Buddy asked to fly with the four. They demurred, saying the plane was a four-seater and there wasn't room. Buddy pleaded; he'd sit on the floor in the rear. The pilot finally caved in and agreed.

Because of Buddy's extra weight the plane ran out of gas before reaching the Hollywood airport and crashed in a Hollywood intersection.

The only one killed was Buddy.

CHAPTER 38

Ralph Flanagan

In 1950, while I was enjoying myself immensely as *Variety*'s Music Editor, I experienced a sudden surge of stupidity. I quit.

Deliberately, I stuck my neck into a circle that would eventually have throttled me if I hadn't, equally suddenly, walked out.

The circle consisted of Herb Hendler, Ralph Flanagan, and the latter's wife, whose name for the life of me I cannot now remember. They brewed a witch's caldron.

The purpose: the construction and promotion of the Ralph Flanagan Orchestra, which, beginning in 1950, became the most sought-after band in the country. In 1951 it grossed slightly over $1,000,000, a figure that few of the major bands of that time ever achieved. Today, that's a pittance for some modern rock combinations, which may reach that number in just one booking in a 50,000-seat ballpark.

It's a weird story. Flanagan, a mouse of a man who yet had guts enough to become a private pilot, was a music arranger. He worked for Mitch Ayres, conductor of the Perry Como Chesterfield TV Orchestra. Living on Long Island, he'd come into New York once a week to deliver musical arrangements, pick up new assignments and his check, and scurry home and repeat the routine.

The launching of the Flanagan band was one of the best promotional jobs ever. Originally an RCA-Victor recordings exec who had left for greener fields, Herb Hendler returned to RCA in 1949 to handle promotion. A deep-dyed Glenn Miller fan, he sold the company on the idea of creating a Miller "sound-alike." The premise was solid. Sales of Miller recordings were dwindling, probably because no new releases were available due to the leader's wartime death.

Hendler argued that a musical copy could: (1) create a "new Miller" or (2) make enough noise using Miller's style or a close approximation of it to stimulate Miller's sales.

He accomplished both objectives.

I came into the picture via Hendler. While on *Variety*, I didn't get along with him, due to his penchant for trying to hide everything he was doing as head of Victor's A & R division, while I made every effort to mine and print whatever I could. We frequently clashed, until a mutual friend got us to bury the hatchet. From then on we were close and many times discussed eventually going into business together.

After we put Flanagan up in front of a band tailor-made by the high-selling Victor recordings Hendler promoted via the wide RCA distributor setup, Flanagan became a nasty bastard with a wife equally well-behaved.

He was from Lorain, Ohio; she from the wrong side of the tracks of Bayonne, New Jersey, where Dick Linke, Andy Griffith's manager, knew her and her back-seat history.

Hendler chose Flanagan to develop a Miller copy because he knew Ralph would follow his ideas implicitly.

The initial RCA recordings released under Flanagan's name actually were studio-made by the Perry Como-Chesterfield Orchestra. They sold well from the very first and kept building because of the disk jockey attention Herb achieved.

The heavy disk-jockey promotion also caused requests for the band to pour into the dozens of ballrooms throughout the East and Midwest.

But each time ballroom owners seeking to hire Flanagan checked booking agency people, they were told there was no Ralph Flanagan Orchestra, that it was a recording band only. Consequently, record sales began to be affected. It behooved us to move quickly.

I left *Variety*. Ralph began rehearsing a band. Herb stayed with RCA as long as he could to push as much as he could promotion-wise. I signed the band to a booking contract with GAC on owner Tom Rockwell's promise that he would deliver a commercial radio broadcast for the band as soon as possible. He did, in 1951—a very lucrative Chesterfield deal that permitted us to air from any place we were working, which enhanced our value to ballroom owners and increased our work opportunities, since the broadcast was done on Monday evenings, normally not a good dance night, if a ballroom operated at all.

However, my problem was how to counter the widely circulated gossip that there was no Ralph Flanagan Orchestra and would not be one.

My close friendship with Frank Dailey, owner of the famed Meadowbrook, Cedar Grove, New Jersey, which seemed to be originating radio broadcasts every time a set was tuned in, was the answer. I sat down with Frank and worked out a March 15, 1950, opening date. He guaranteed 23 network-broadcasts-a-week, which we figured would convince anyone interested that the Flanagan band was for real.

The band took off like a rocket, the money rolled in, and the fun began.

Flanagan, we found, was a hit bandleader who loved the money but hated being a bandleader. He and his wife were both low-class people who added stupid, often unbelievable problems to the normal, everyday difficulties of managing and moving around the country a group of 18 musicians and singers.

Since Ralph loved money and wanted to reap it as fast as possible, I worked the band for 17 consecutive months without a single day off, except when we played "locations" or hotel dates when, according to AFM rules, the musicians got a day off each week.

A head-shrinker would have had a ball with Ralph. There was no fathoming what ate this man, whether (1) the success of the band as hand-made for him by Hendler bugged him, or (2) he resented knowing he was trading on Glenn Miller's reputation, or (3) that he would have much preferred to be safe at home.

I've known intimately a number of bandleaders topmost in popularity, but none as stupid, as bull-headed, and as inconsiderate as Flanagan. He seemed to do everything he could to alienate customers, the fans, the ones who pay the freight. He had more dumb tricks than a birthday magician and, more often than not, was meaner than the proverbial junk-yard dog. The man simply did not know how to be nice to anyone.

One of Flanagan's favorite tricks he reserved for fans. Most bandstands are shoulder-level higher than the dance floor. When Ralph noticed someone approaching to talk to him, he'd turn around to "conduct," hoping he or she would go away. Trying to get his attention, often a fan would pull on his pants leg, whereupon Flanagan would kick backward on the pretext his leg was caught on something. Often his kick would end in the face of the fan. I saw him kick a girl in the teeth in Albuquerque. She had to control her boyfriend from pulling Flanagan off the stand.

And his wife out-did Ralph at every turn. Whenever anything went wrong, which had to happen in so complex an operation, her favorite crack to Herb or me, but most gleefully to our wives if they were present, was, "Well, back to the salt mines for you guys," which meant we all were headed for the "squalor" from which we came before we transformed her husband from a mouse who didn't like to leave his hole into a successful bandleader.

Plus which, this gal was always on the make. One night, with Flanagan just beginning a dance set at Meadowbrook, she made a pass at me in his dressing room. I fluffed her off. She got furious.

There has always been a suspicion Herb Hendler kept her happy though (he'd fuck anything that came within a yard of him). Years after I quit the band my wife told me that once, when we'd spent a weekend with Herb and his wife of the time, he had suggested to her that we switch partners. He and his gal, Tommy, a wonderful human being whom Lorraine and I loved, almost split when Herb and Ralph's wife got staggering drunk together at the wedding of Clare and Buddy Morrow (whose band we also managed) and disappeared for a few hours. This was after Clare, a fashion model, pointedly asked Ralph's spouse to leave the reception because her behavior was so disruptive.

It was hard to tell when Flanagan was nastiest—sober or dead drunk. His wife, however, let it all hang out when she'd had a few blasts. I booked the band into the Palladium Ballroom, Hollywood, opening late in January 1951. Herb and Tommy flew out and Lorraine and I later took the Twentieth-Century and the Chief. I needed the rest the three-day train ride provided.

In Hollywood, Tom Rockwell, who usually spent the winter at his agency's West Coast office, invited us all to his home in Duarte, then to dinner at Newman's Steak House, on the side of a mountain above the Monrovia-Duarte-Azusa area. The minute we got to Tom's we got into the booze. And when the place began to rock we cooled it and took off for dinner.

Tom sat at the head of the table. Lorraine, whom he liked immensely, was on his right and Flanagan's wife on his left. Herb's wife was next to Lorraine. Vivian, Rockwell's wife, a great lady accustomed to and immune to the fun and foibles any coterie of artists and their managers could produce, was at the other end with Ralph, Herb and me.

I heard a commotion. Flanagan's wife was wiping her face. She had pulled her infamous "salt mines" line on Lorraine and Tommy in front of Rockwell, and my wife had flung a glass of Scotch in her face, ice and all. Tom sat there unconcerned. Flanagan got up and seemed to indicate he would be less than a mouse this time around. I headed for him. Vivian, almost an Amazon, simply picked me up and walked me to one side, meanwhile whispering it all wasn't worth the trouble.

In the middle of all this, Flanagan loudly announced he was going to the bathroom. Consistent with his rebellious personality, he wasn't going to the men's room, he was going outside to help Newman's plants weather the dry spell. He disappeared and didn't come back. Herb and I went looking for him and found him face down in his own piss.

That did it; nobody ate. Herb and Tommy climbed into the back of our rental and Lorraine and I got in the front, preparing to drive down the mountain on a dirt road that had no side rails. The dropoff was around 1,000 feet. Flanagan and his wife headed for the brand-new Packard he'd had delivered in Hollywood that week. (Consistent with everything else he did, Flanagan drove outmoded cars. He'd traded a Studebaker on the Packard.) When I saw him having difficulty getting into the car I began to grin. I held a $100,000 insurance policy on the guy and here he was, dead drunk, about to negotiate a road with a 1,000-foot drop and no railing.

Lorraine saw what I was thinking.

"He'll kill himself and her. Get him out from behind that wheel," she screamed at me. She was right. I couldn't let him do it. I tossed him in my back seat after the usual mumbled "I'll-drive-my-own-car" routine. All the way down the mountain and into Hollywood, I let his wife have both barrels. For once she knew she'd started something uglier than usual. She also knew that Herb and I could destroy the guy in the back seat and backed off. Not completely. Once things again got as smooth as they'd ever get, she was back at the old stand.

There was constant turmoil around the band. Flanagan wasn't choosy about whom he tried to ride roughshod—musicians, agents, stagehands, fans, even disk jockeys on occasion, which was like biting the hand.

And Flanagan was a bigot. In the fall of 1951 I set up a package "concert" deal involving our band and the Mills Brothers, without question the greatest singing group ever to hit the enter-

tainment business. The deal called for four one-nighters in
Michigan auditoriums. It was a great show, which finally gave me
a chance to use my *Variety*-earned expertise re production.

After the dates were set up, Tom Rockwell, head of GAC,
which also booked the Mills group, called and asked me whether
the Mills men could ride in our bus from one date to the next. I
said, "Sure, why not?"

Flanagan refused and I had to eat my words.

The band was only a couple weeks old when we were in trouble
with the American Federation of Musicians. Rehearsing for a
radio broadcast, Flanagan was in the booth trying to balance
sound. He didn't like the bassist he had hired. To embarrass the
guy, he shouted via the mike, "Is that your bass I hear or are you
kicking the wall?"

There was an AFM rep in the studio Flanagan didn't see.
That's all, brother.

The kid was induced to press charges. There is an AFM rule
that one member cannot "put down" another's performance. It
took me months and a lot of maneuvering to get him out from
under that one. Bandleaders, though they also are AFM members,
got short shrift in a case involving a sideman musician.

Flanagan got into trouble with the FAA, not once but twice and
finally had his pilot's license lifted. On one road trip through Iowa
Ralph decided to fly, which usually was difficult since ballrooms
and airport locations do not always coincide. I had come out from
New York (for the first year or so either Herb or I was with the band
at all times, obviously to protect our interests) and flew along on
each date in the Ryan he owned at the time. One afternoon we
reached the area of that night's dance and spotted our bus along-
side a lake. The men were swimming. Flanagan buzzed them

twice. In the pattern to land, I spotted a police cruiser entering the airport. The officer was waiting, book in hand, when we pulled up.

It took months to get Flanagan out of that scrape. The FAA didn't believe our story that we dropped down to check where we were, since we had buzzed twice.

That's not the last time I found that flying with Flanagan might be risky. We were going into the Steel Pier, Atlantic City. Herb dreamed up the idea of scattering advertising leaflets from Flanagan's plane. He knew there was an ordinance against littering and an arrest would make the papers and mention the Steel Pier. I went along to toss out the leaflets.

Afterward, Ralph flew up and down, just off the beach. I was taking motion pictures. Looking through the lens I saw what looked like a string go by the wing-tip. I dropped the camera and looked back. The "string" was the steel cable that anchored a miniature blimp the Pier always kept in the air to attract attention. Ralph wouldn't believe me until I had the films developed and ran them off for him. He'd never noticed the cable.

Another one of his roughshod stunts could have cost him his life. I was no longer with the band, but the story was told to me by Henry Miller, GAC West Coast exec. Booked into Vandenberg Air Force base, California, the home of highly classified equipment, Flanagan decided to fly in—without mentioning it to anyone. He had a gnat-sized Mooney by then. As he approached the field he was advised by radio to veer off, private planes were verboten. Base controllers assumed he was tuned. He was, but turned down his radio and kept coming. Anti-aircraft guns were about to blow him out of the sky when someone with binoculars read the band name on the side of the little plane.

Ralph had another episode with the Mooney. Taking off from Chicago's Midway, he was advised by the tower to wait for an airliner coming in, then go. Checking, he felt he could be airborne before the airliner arrived. The Mooney apparently has difficulty getting out of its own way. It didn't get out of the liner's way. The newspaper version was that the big ship flew right over the Mooney and, when it blasted reverse power to slow, the Mooney was blown sky high and came down on its back. All Flanagan got was a bad knee.

One really bad scene was not caused by Ralph for once, but he ultimately contributed by riding roughshod over a stagehand. That's a no-no guaranteed to draw fire and brimstone—or at least a sandbag from overhead flies over the theatre stage.

During the third show, a CBS page advised me that a gentleman insisted on seeing me immediately and would not wait for the end of the show. The guy handed me a bill for $226 on a National Variety Artists billhead.

"For what?" I asked.

"For moving the band in and out of this theater for the past three weeks," was the answer.

"You didn't do that," I came back. "What is this, a holdup?"

The NVA rep explained they had a contract with all New York theaters to move everything going in and out of theater-studios. Knowing nothing except a principle, I refused to pay for work not done. The NVA tried every which way to get me to pay the bill.

"You'll pay," they stated.

Ultimately, I went to Flanagan's union, the American Federation of Musicians. Its prez, James C. Petrillo, told me bluntly on the phone, "Woods, if you pay those motherfuckers one thin dime, I'll tear up Flanagan's card." So, I refused to cave in until we were booked into the Capitol Theater, New York, which was running band shows in opposition to the Paramount and Strand theaters on Broadway.

The first weekend at the Cap, the manager asked me to join him in his office. There were two NVA men there. He stepped out. I was told bluntly that they knew where I lived in Bayside, knew I had a wife and two youngsters, and insisted that I pay the months-old bill. (I had already paid to move into the Capitol, a job done legitimately, with which I had no quarrel.)

I'd had enough.

I asked the NVA men to come to my office the next day. I paid them in cash and from my office they phoned Dan Tobin, head of the teamsters union of which the NVA was a part. Tobin offered me a deal. "If you work that CBS studio or any other again, park your bus around the corner and have your men dolly your equipment to the job," he said, "and we won't bother you."

I was flabbergasted, but agreed. Later that spring, GAC booked us for a television broadcast out of the old studio on 53rd Street. To make it, the band had to suffer an all-night bus run and got to the theater about 10 a.m.

I was in the office, Herb was at the studio. He called and screamed, "Get your ass over here quick, all hell has broken loose." I was there in ten minutes, just in time to receive Dan Tobin's livid phone call.

"You violated our deal," he yelled.

"We did like hell," I shouted back.

"Your bus was at the door," he retorted. "Not only that, but your leader tried to injure one of my men." This last I couldn't believe, but I'd had no time to question anyone before picking up his call.

I called for Dan Gregory, our road manager, and was told the bus had been at the door.

"Your men will be paid," I told Tobin and hung up.

Then I found that Flanagan, hazy on the details of the deal I had made with Tobin, had gotten angry when the truckers tried to move our equipment into the theater. He picked up a drum case himself and, when a Tobin man tried to stop him, he simply used the case as a battering ram, knocked the man down and walked over him and into the theater.

The stagehands, a different union, but union nonetheless, took a dim view of Flanagan's action. That's when the sandbag from the flies above hit the stage a foot or two from Flanagan's head and the shit hit the fan.

I finally straightened the whole thing out with three cases of booze—one Scotch, one rye, and one gin. We put on a dilly of a TV show.

I didn't really care about Flanagan's head. I still carried that insurance on him.

Mentioning Flanagan's head brings to mind the funny story that happened during my tenure with the band. We were in Phoenix, to work a college date. Flanagan and I went to a barber shop and, since we both were very tired, almost went to sleep in the chair. I came to a bit later, glanced at Ralph, and almost fell out of my chair. His barber had given him a close cut, not realizing that the hair he was snipping was a rug—a hairpiece. He was partially bald. And it was the only one he had.

Flanagan could get himself and, very often, all those around him into hot water. At breakfast, he'd love to scan the menu and order "#2—with three eggs." (Then a three-egg deal was unusual. Today it's common.)

"That comes with two eggs," the waitress would come back. "But, I want three eggs."

The average waitress would stand there with her mouth open. She had never had to think before. Finally, she'd say, "That's a set breakfast. I wouldn't know what to charge you; the boss isn't here."

"Charge me anything, but get me three eggs."

"I can't," the waitress would wail. "Please go somewhere else."

If you're diet conscious, it's a sure way to stay on track. By the time the argument is settled you're no longer hungry.

Flanagan had other noneating habits. In a restaurant, he'd file his order. If the service was slow, he'd wait until he saw what he thought was his meal approaching, then get up and leave. Both he and his wife did that to Herb and me and our wives in one of the best hotels in Atlantic City. We were embarrassed no end trying to explain.

I missed going to jail in Fort Wayne, Indiana, by an eyelash due to a similar trick. I had come out from New York with some things for Flanagan's signature and to pick up new band arrangements he had written on the road. After the dance we were told there was only one place to eat. We headed there. The place was jammed with kids from the dance, but we got two seats at the counter while I found an empty chair at a table behind me to park my brief case.

Since the place was packed, we had to wait. Finally, we ordered. More waiting. When Flanagan saw the waitress exit from the kitchen with what he thought was our food, he slid off his stool and out the door. She placed both plates. When his obviously wasn't being touched, she asked me where he was.

"I have no idea," I said. "He was just an acquaintance."

Finishing, I turned to pick up my brief case. It was gone. One of the guys at that table told me the cashier had it.

"I have it and you're not getting it unless you pay your friend's tab," he said.

The case contained contracts and tapes Flanagan had made of new arrangements for Herb's consideration, new scores—all irreplaceable material.

"You're nuts," I told the guy. "I'm not responsible for his tab and the things you're holding belong to me. Give them up or I'll call the cops."

"Go—there's a phone," he said.

Two cops answered my call. One, after hearing the owner's story and being told who Flanagan was, kept insisting they should run me in for "disorderly conduct." I told him he wasn't too bright, which infuriated the flatfoot. His partner, with a little more smarts, checked the contents of the brief case and, finding mail addressed to me, plus other identification, advised the cashier to return my property.

When I got back to the hotel where Flanagan and I were sharing a room, he was sleeping like a baby. I had to resist the urge to conk him with a bedside lamp.

I mentioned Flanagan wanted money—as fast as possible. I was in Hollywood with the band, our second date at the Palladium. I got a call from our New York accountant. He advised me that checks Ralph had signed and I countersigned before leaving New York were doing a bouncing ball act. I told him that was impossible, to check the bank. He called back and told me that the account was almost clean because Ralph, without telling anyone, had removed $30,000, leaving only a few hundred available. I grabbed him. He admitted he had removed "his" money to buy a piece of real estate.

I was forced to go to Tom Rockwell and borrow $10,000 until the account could be built back up. He was flabbergasted at having to supply coin to one of the most financially successful bands he'd been associated with over the years.

To me, that was the capper. Between a nut of a bandleader, the leader's vitriolic, moronic wife, and a partner who would fuck or drink anything he could lay hands on (he had a pal, drafted into service for the Korean conflict. While the guy was in, Herb did him a favor—he serviced his wife), I figured the whole thing was not worth it. The stress was making me make mistakes. And Lorraine was bugging me to get out. She cared not one whit for the money involved.

I quit. I told Herb I wanted out. I had a ten-year contract with over eight still to run. As a means of extricating myself quickly I asked for $25,000, which was ridiculously low in view of the earning capacity of the band.

Within a year after ridding myself of that trio, I had a number of good acts under contract, which made me a great living. I led a much more placid existence. The management business was tough enough without having to deal with nasty, drunken associates.

CHAPTER 39

Bobby Vinton

I've had some wild and woolly experiences with major and minor singers while on *Variety* and later in management. By far the weirdest was with the "Polish Prince"—Bobby Vinton. He originally was the lead singer in a group called the Tempos, which I managed for a few years in the 50's.

Bobby had left the group before I showed up and was working in a Canonsburg, Pennsylvania, factory, his and Perry Como's hometown. He came to New York on occasion with the Tempos and I got to know him.

One evening Bobby called me at home, explaining that a backer was willing to put up the money for a recording session. He asked whether I would set it up for him. I agreed, on the condition that I would receive a management contract. We agreed in principle over several more calls and I went ahead.

I really had never heard Bobby sing but I was assured by
Tempo members that he had a voice for the modern market. Thus
I was eager to do what I could to help. As a manager one could
never really predict with certainty public reaction to anything. So,
one tried all the holes.

The only fly in the ointment, Bobby explained, was that his
backer could not or would not put up in advance the money
required for a deposit on the musicians' salaries, as required by
New York Local 802 of the American Federation of Musicians.

That sounded a bit off base, but I went ahead.

On my reputation, Al Knopf, an 802 executive, waived the
deposit rule and I proceeded. Eddie Kissack, record producer
under Jimmy Hilliard at RCA's subsidiary, Label X, a close friend,
was to be in Cleveland for daytime recording. But he made plans to
fly in, handle the date for me, then fly back. He was a crackerjack.

I set up everything, hired 16 musicians from the Perry Como
TV orchestra, all standouts, and reserved a Capitol Records studio, right opposite *Variety's* New York offices.

Bobby called the morning before and advised he was ready. He
was to bring the arrangements with him and call me when he got
into the hotel that night. He didn't call, but the omission didn't
bother me since I knew Pittsburgh-to-New York air travel then
wasn't always dependable weather-wise.

The next morning I went to my office first, knowing it would
be awhile until the musicians "ran down" Bobby's material.

The phone rang. It was Kissack. The band was warmed and
ready to go.

"Where's Bobby?" he asked.

"If he's not there, I don't know," was my brilliant answer.

I called the hotel. Bobby hadn't checked in. I called his
Canonsburg number. Bobby picked up the phone instantly and I

dropped mine. When I recovered and with a mental picture of musicians, engineers, and an A & R man twiddling their thumbs while the clock went round and round, killing perhaps a $10 bill with each tick, I screamed, "What the hell are you doing in Canonsburg?"

Dead silence. After I thought he'd quietly hung up, came Bobby's voice.

"I couldn't make it," he whimpered.

"What the hell do you mean you couldn't make it?" I bellowed, on the verge of apoplexy.

Bobby was almost crying when he explained that the friend who promised him the money for the session wouldn't or couldn't come through. He was a bookie and the day Bobby was to leave for New York he said he'd been cleaned out, driven stone broke by a long-shot some smart operators had put over. Other books were broken, too, Bobby said.

Whether the story was true or not I never did find out. I knew that when books even have a glimmer of suspicion they can lay off almost any amounts. Apparently, Bobby's man couldn't smell a rat. He blew the whole wad, so he said.

I had to call the studio and cancel everything. Then I had to go to Al Knopf and explain that a "boat race" ran me up the creek.

I don't believe I've seen or heard from Vinton to this day.

A few years later, Vinton made it to the studio on schedule and began the series of recordings that turned him from a welsher into the Polish Prince. Whether that would have happened as a result of the session that didn't happen only heaven knows.

The music business has long since learned that a song or an artist successful today might not have "happened" a few years earlier or a few years later. So, perhaps the whole thing worked to Vinton's advantage.

It sure wasn't to mine.

Mentioning the Tempos brings to mind a short story that epitomizes the problems managers go through with artists for the 10 or
20 percent they draw and why the sneering term "flesh peddler"
is far, far off the mark.

I had high hopes for the Tempos. It featured a lead singer with
a voice like a calliope, somewhat akin to Frankie Valli's later hit
style with the Four Seasons. From demos, I signed them to a contract with Paris Records, owned by Jack Gold, later to head the
Columbia Records Hollywood office.

Sherman Edwards, a songwriter friend from my *Variety* days,
who later wrote the Broadway smash, "1776", dug into his trunk
and came up with a song titled "See You in September." The
record became a hit, taking off in sales after we did the Dick
Clark show at WCAU, Philadelphia.

While the record was building I was dickering to sign the
group to GAC, which provided a few bookings as talks pro-
gressed. When the contract was ready, I sent it to the kids who in
turn sent it to a Pittsburgh attorney.

A short time later I received a call from this attorney. "Mr.
Woods," he said, "I cannot in good conscience permit the Tempos
to sign the GAC contract unless you cancel, in writing to me, your
contract with them."

When I came down I told him flatly there was no way I was
going to do that; whatever strides this group had taken in show-
business had been generated by me. I made the demo which got
them the record contract, I found the song that was letting them
rise above the crowd. I had gotten them work through independent agents while the GAC contract was being worked out, etc.

Only then did my temper subside enough to ask on what he
based his attitude.

"The GAC contract uses the word management and so does yours. I cannot permit that conflict," he explained.

I pointed out that one pact said "management of bookings" while the other said "personal management." That meant two different things. I explained that the industry had lived for years under those descriptions without problems. His answer was still the same. He adamantly refused further discussion.

Since the act was not working much because even GAC wouldn't continue to book them without a contract, Jack Gold lost interest in a second record and I didn't push him.

"See you in September" sold about 500,000 copies, big numbers in those days, and the song itself became a "standard." It was recorded by a different group every spring for years afterward.

The Tempos? They blithely sided with their attorney and sat watching a promising career go down the drain. Whether for some reason they'd come to disagree with me as a manager and chose this way of getting rid of me, I never did fathom. But my contract was in effect for several years afterward and I never heard of them again.

Oh, yes I did. At least two, including the calliope kid, were working in Pittsburgh factories.

CHAPTER 40

J. Fred Muggs

Perhaps the craziest thing I ever got into during my days in personal management was handling an ape.

Lunching one day with Dee Belline, Perry Como's brother-in-law, Dee asked whether I was open to the idea of handling an animal act. After considering it, I answered, "Why not?"

Dee explained he was friendly with the owners of J. Fred Muggs, the chimp that had been featured for some time on the early-morning Dave Garroway show on NBC. The chimp was leaving the show and figured to be worth booking after so long a TV exposure.

I met with Muggs' owners and we struck a deal. I'll never forget that first afternoon. We'd completed discussions and the two owners and the chimp and I headed for the van they owned, parked on Broadway. So here I am waltzing up the main drag with a chimp hand-in-hand. He was very quiet.

We reached the van, and the first thing Muggs did was dive into the glove compartment, which held fruit Lifesavers, which he loved. One of the owners took them away, explaining Muggs was soon to have "dinner" and the candy would ruin his appetite. The chimp went off like a rocket. His screaming was unearthly. He screamed and screamed like he was being killed, jumping in and out of the car. It was rush hour and we began to be noticed, to say the least. I got a bit leery.

One of the handlers belted him in the chops at the top of a jump in the driver's seat and Muggs did three somersaults into the back seat, then sat complacently looking out the window. He never uttered another sound. I was shook.

Other than a few supermarket appearances there wasn't much that could be done with Muggs. He did not have a repertoire of stunts. When Garroway's producers wanted something special for the next day's show, the handlers would teach what was required overnight and all was well.

So, my chimp connection didn't last too long.

CHAPTER 41

Boyd Raeburn

Boyd Raeburn was no bigger than a minute. When he tooted his baritone sax, it sometimes was difficult to see him. But he was a dynamo who almost always headed a very acceptable orchestra, featuring vocals by his wife, Ginny Powell, a highly respected singer, who strangely stuttered badly when she wasn't singing.

The first time I reviewed Boyd's orchestra was on his opening in the Century Room of the New York Commodore Hotel. The band had been operating mostly in the Midwest, out of Chicago. It worked with such verve that I opened the review with a real smart-aleck remark. I said, "Boyd Raeburn does not have to worry about losing his Midwestern fans. They can hear him every time he climbs on this bandstand, with or without a broadcast wire."

That was the only connection I had with Boyd until years later. Around 1955, Boyd and Ginny were living in New York. I'd run into them occasionally. Then he approached me on the idea of building a new band, outlining what he had in mind. I agreed with most of his thoughts and we proceeded.

He had an excellent arranger named Stan Applebaum.

The new band worked numerous one-nighters out of New York and began doing well financially. But it was headed for slow death since it didn't have a recording contract, without which no new venture could long succeed. I went to Columbia Records, where Mitch Miller had just taken on the A & R chair after moving over from Mercury Records.

I knew Mitch well after a wild experience with him. He had been with Mercury in Chicago and the company moved him to New York. He called me at *Variety* and asked if I would come to his office (I did the record reviews then). When I did he played me a tremendous recording by Frankie Laine that I flipped over. It was titled "Mule Train." I didn't know it then, but Miller was being clever. Using me. The song came from a then unreleased Vaughn Monroe western. I believe it was the only film Monroe ever made. And Vaughn had not yet recorded the song for RCA-Victor.

Mitch wanted to release Laine's, but couldn't without permission from the publisher (Disney). And Disney was reluctant to okay Laine's version until Monroe's was ready.

So, Mitch figured to use force. He told me I could review the disk. I did. I also shouted loud and long about Laine's great new record around Lindy's. Disney executives finally gave in and okayed the Laine version for release. To compete with a recording of a song from his own film Monroe was forced to do a hurry-up version that didn't come within miles of Laine's exciting arrangement.

Mitch gave me a contract for Raeburn calling for four sides. But, he couldn't be involved. He had just moved into the A & R spot and was busy trying to revive Columbia Records, then in such dire straits its parent, Columbia Broadcasting, was about to throw in the towel and sell it off.

Therefore, Mitch had little time for Raeburn. He turned us over to George Avakian, a producer then more involved with jazz. George had no time for us either. He did something I'd never heard of before, but which is prevalent in today's recording. He told me to get everything together and when we were ready he'd assign a studio and a control room engineer. We were on our own.

I got together two standard songs for Ginny, who was not about to be left out of any recording activity, and two instrumentals that we dug up from a Harlem arranger.

At that time, rock was beginning to make noise. The "thing" was a heavy beat. So, when we recorded I had the engineer place mikes to allow Boyd's drummer to use his drum cases instead of the drums, both beneath the full band and in solos. We made four sides that knocked me out and did the same for Avakian when he went over them. They were modern in sound and they swung like mad.

A week later Mitch called me and advised that Columbia could not release the sides we had made. They conflicted with an idea he had been developing for a bandleader on the label with whom he was closely allied. (It never worked out. I still believe he wanted to appropriate the idea.)

So, another good effort went down the drain. But, as they say, that's show biz.

CHAPTER 42

Brock Peters

A while back I saw a boxed item in a San Francisco newspaper detailing the names of entertainers who became stars after winning top honors on Arthur Godfrey's "Talent Scout" TV show on CBS in the 50's.

It gave me a nostalgic laugh.

In the 50's I came across singer Brock Peters, a huge young man with a great bass voice. He was more of a calypso singer on the order of Harry Belafonte. I put him under contract and began trying to open doors.

Along the way, I got the idea of submitting him to Godfrey's show. He was accepted. Then I determined through friends that we could make him a winner—simply by coming up with $200 cash, no checks.

I got the cash and Brock came up with the win (which he was not aware of).

The routine was simple. The contestants were judged by the volume of applause from the studio audience. When all the "amateur" entertainers had their shot, Godfrey held a hand over the head of each while an applause meter in the control room registered volume.

But the mikes were controlled by audio-meters, or pots, on the control board. All one had to do was open or close them to get a desired result. And for $200 they were open all the way for Brock.

Brock went on to much bigger things. Through GAC and an agent named Artie Price, Brock was signed for a part in the musical film *Carmen Jones*. Then a role with Sammy Davis in *Porgy and Bess*. We parted after that for I had no desire to move to Hollywood and he wanted to move from Brooklyn and make his home there.

Among the many acting roles he's had since, his greatest was in *To Kill a Mockingbird* with Gregory Peck, a film high on the list of Oscar winners.

CHAPTER 43

Richard Maltby

One of the arranger/bandleaders I became involved with in the middle 50's was well known in musical circles as an arranger for a number of the top bands. After some of his work furthered the reputations of other bandleaders, Richard Maltby concluded he could do the same for himself. So he sought to set up a band of his own.

I agreed with his ideas, though physically Maltby was not the epitome of a bandleader type. He looked more like a chubby accountant than a well-schooled musical personality.

Richard put a band together. We shook the band down by playing one-nighters, all within driving distance of New York. I secured a summer-replacement television show, on which the band did well. In the fall we began widening our booking sphere.

Through GAC, to which I'd signed the band, we picked up a term booking in Chicago. Richard and I, plus his close friend who was to become his road manager, drove overnight and checked into the Sherman Hotel in the early afternoon.

I was expecting to hit the sack since I had driven a fair portion of the way.

Richard turned to me and asked, "Where's the broads?"

I brightly asked, "What broads?" thinking he was kidding.

"Hell," he answered, "you've been on the road for a number of years. You must have a book of numbers as long as your arm. Let's go, let's go."

I didn't produce. Richard got really bent out of shape at my inability to satisfy his wants and in a short while we split. Then he got mixed up with his vocalist. Then he got divorced from a really nice woman.

I guess I was not a good manager.

CHAPTER 44

Louis Jordan

After I cut out of the Flanagan setup I managed a number of bandleaders and/or arrangers. One of the craziest I got involved with afforded me as much cranial trouble as Flanagan, although I did very well with him financially.

This was Louis Jordan, a former Chick Webb saxophonist who formed a small combo that did excellent things on Decca Records. He was like Flanagan in that he felt he could do anything he wanted whether or not it hurt others or agreed with people more or less in control.

When I picked him up via my and his accountant, Phil Braunstein, Louis was on the downgrade. But he had enough left in personality and performance to enable me to book him on television shows as well as on road and club dates.

Louis had been high on the hog for a number of years as a result of record hits like "Caldonia," and had gone through a very rough time with a first wife who crossed him to the point he did-n't trust anyone. That, in all likelihood, caused the breakup with his previous manager.

It was often obvious Louis didn't trust me either.

In his earlier days, Louis had written a number of instrumen-tal tunes, among them "Caldonia," and his wife, without his knowledge, had copyrighted them in her name. When they broke up, she waltzed off with his poke, so to speak.

Louis would do such things as he did one February—close a Reno club run and have two days to drive to Chicago to open at the Aragon Ballroom. Normally, that would be no problem. But, without telling me, he had arranged to play a dance date in Texas, to help out a promoter friend who needed money. Then, with less than twenty hours to complete the run, he tried for the Chicago opening. No expressways, nothing but icy two-lane roads most of the way. Naturally, he didn't come close.

The manager (me) took the brunt of the resultant explosion. The Aragon was an important date.

What caused Louis and me to say *arrivederci*, however, was a dilly of a deal that I don't believe any manager, booking agency, or recording exec ever heard of before or since.

At this point, Louis Jordan was a cold duck on records. Decca had released him and I couldn't get any junior label interested, until Herman Diaz took over Label X, RCA-Victor's label. Herman bought my pitch on Louis and the combo was signed to a four-record deal. He was assigned tunes selected by Diaz for a recording date a few weeks hence during a week's run at the Apollo Theater in Harlem. The recording was to be done at RCA's 24th Street studio.

The night prior to recording I went up to the Apollo and Louis got his men together between shows to give me a rundown of the arrangements of the songs assigned. They were excellent. I had high hopes.

The recording was set for 10 a.m.

Jordan walked into that studio and tried to force upon Diaz four songs that no one had ever heard of. Overnight he had run into some Harlem songwriters (either that or his performance for me of the assigned songs was a sham) who offered him 50 percent of the copyrights if he would record songs they had written. Since he had lost all the value of his previous copyrights when his wife absconded, Louis figured to start building a new portfolio by ramming the new songs down the throat of RCA-Victor recording executives.

While Louis was rehearsing the kinks out of the first song, Herman kept asking what was going on, this was not one of the songs assigned. It was difficult for him to believe me when I said I had no idea what Jordan was trying to do, since I'd previously raved about the arrangements of the songs he'd been assigned and had "run down" for me.

Jordan continued to go over "his" songs for an hour while Herman and I tried to turn him in the right direction.

Finally, we'd both had enough. Diaz simply turned off all recording equipment, doused the studio lights, and we walked out, leaving the Louis Jordan group in the dark.

I never saw or spoke with him again.

CHAPTER 45

Disappearance

What happened to the Big Bands? Why did they all but disappear in the late 40's and early 50's? My own theory, after having lived and worked through it all, has two arguments to it:

(1) The Second World War

(2) Frank Sinatra

When the Japanese jumped Pearl Harbor in 1941 the youth of the nation lined up for military service, which, of course, took thousands out of their preferred "service"—escorting girls to dances.

At the height of the Big Band madness, males were much more attracted to the many great bandleader names and their music than were the girls. The girls just went along with the boys since they were boys.

Then the boys went one way, the girls another, the boys into service, while most of the girls stayed put and pined.

283

As the war escalated and more and more men disappeared into uniform, the situation became more serious. Fewer and fewer couples meant less income at the ballroom or club box-office. Ladies then didn't always go to dances alone.

At the same time, Big Band operating costs down the line began to increase. The main mode of movement for all traveling bands during the Big Band Era was leased buses. Fuel costs went up. Hotel prices went up. Musicians needed higher salaries to subsist (they paid their own expenses on the road). Therefore, the major Big Band names were forced to increase one-night prices, which forced ballroom operators to boost box-office tolls.

The usual cause and effect.

Like Topsy, the whole thing grew and grew until virtually all Big Bands were forced to the edge of pricing themselves out of business.

History tells us that one "era" always leads to another. Frank Sinatra's decision to leave Tommy Dorsey and solo helped. He teed off the Singer's Era. His performances with Dorsey had been stirring up the gals as no other singer in the history of show-business—including Bing Crosby, who was then everyone's favorite, both male and female.

Frank stole the girls. Turned their heads from the Big Bands. Riots wherever he appeared (I got caught in several). He simply siphoned off a great deal of the attention young people formerly gave to the bandleaders. Naturally the bands suffered.

Frank's unbelievable success set it up for others such as Perry Como, who actually began gathering his own flock of followers at almost the same time but who was without question overshadowed. And there were others behind P.C., outstanding voices in their own right, but none with the style and sexy gliss that put Frank in power.

Plus which Frank proved to be an excellent actor, strengthening his grip on a tremendous career.

Como and perhaps Tony Bennett have come closest to Sinatra's long-term hold on his fans. Bennett is still working. His management and he himself were very astute, cleverly building his reputation one brick at a time until he was solidly entrenched. Clearly, his vocal approach was and is different than Frank's and he smartly did not try to imitate, as did so many others. Como and his management group achieved the same results. But, he was not an actor, proven by the one crack he had at Hollywood.

Vic Damone, whom I deem the most vocally talented of all, tried to ape Frank's style at the outset. One of his first important dates was the Century Room of the now-defunct Commodore Hotel, New York. I reviewed his performance and disagreed with his attempted Sinatra sound-alike, as did others. Soon after, Vic decided to become Vic and his rep began to build. He is still the best. But, he's also weak on acting.

Jimmy Van Heusen, the songwriter, once told me a great story about Damone. On his first booking on the Coast, he worked Ciro's. As usual, when a new kid shows up on the block of stars, the Hollywood gals like to try him out. Ava Gardner made a date with Vic (before Sinatra) and went to Ciro's to pick him up. She was waiting at the bar when Vic walked up.

"Have a drink?" Ava offered.

"I don't drink," said Vic.

"Have a cigarette?" Ava suggested.

"I don't smoke," came back Vic.

Ava gathered up her purse and cigs and cracked, "I'll bet you don't fuck either," as she stalked off.

There were others as great or better than Frank from a strict voice-ability, but they didn't have an intriguing style, didn't get the breaks, or whatever. Dick Haymes, who worked with Tommy Dorsey for awhile was up near the top voice-wise, got many breaks, but could not reach that pinnacle, at least as a singer.

Jack Jones was another great, voice-wise, who didn't realize his potential, for one reason or another.

Another outstanding voice performer was Bob Eberly, who sang with Jimmy Dorsey all of his band career. Bob had a powerful, attractive baritone. But he was given the shaft by Jimmy's personal manager, Bill Burton, my close friend—so close then he became my first son's godfather, despite the fact that he was Jewish and I and my wife Roman Catholic.

After Bob's huge hits with Jimmy on "Green Eyes," "Amapola," and "My Prayer," he unquestionably was in a strong position to be launched as a single. He was impatient, I know.

Burton convinced him to wait, that the time was not ripe. "Let it build a little more," he said.

Some time later Jimmy Dorsey was booked into the huge Roxy Theater, New York, which was attempting a Big Band policy, and I was assigned to review the show. Almost the instant Bob opened his mouth I knew something was wrong. Burton, whom I'd spoken to the night before, hadn't mentioned a cold or anything else bothering Bob or Jimmy or any of his people.

Bob's voice never again reached its former power. Later the reason, in my opinion, surfaced. A short time before the Roxy opening Burton had signed Dick Haymes to a personal management contract and Eberly became aware of the move. At almost the same time Bob received "Greetings" from the government. And his wife was pregnant.

That combination of events, particularly Burton's obvious and perfidious defection, plus the government's beckoning finger, apparently worked on Bob and his voice suffered, I have heard him a number of times since, in the local clubs he played around New York and New Jersey, and his voice was never the same.

That's really a tough rap because he was clearly one of the best.

Burton's excuse for being so blatant as to sign Haymes in the face of all the promises he had made to Eberly was, to me, unacceptable, but I could understand it to some degree. There is no question that Eberly's work with Helen O'Connell was the major reason for the popularity of the Jimmy Dorsey Orchestra despite the excellence of its musical performance. Every hit recording by the band was a hit because of the vocals. None at that time were instrumental until "So Rare," late in Jimmy's career.

Simply, what Burton sought to do by conning Eberly into staying with the band as long as possible, was to protect Jimmy Dorsey's future, thereby protecting his own. As close as I was to Burton I had no knowledge of his financial arrangement with Jimmy. But he must have had a nice piece. He spent money recklessly.

There were other great singers among male band vocalists. One I particularly loved to listen to was Billy Eckstine. He had an unusual baritone voice and a way with lyrics that knocked me out.

There were many more outstanding singers among the girls than among the men, however, and not all the successful ones came out of bands of the era.

Dinah Shore, for example, never to my knowledge worked with a Big Band. Conversely, her biggest break came after making that one single recording with Xavier Cugat's Orchestra.

Another great one among the girls who never got a break at all was Helen Forrest. This gal was more facile vocally than many of her rivals and, what was important then (and still is), when she sang one could understand every word.

Then we get to perhaps the greatest in her groove—Ella Fitzgerald. She has had all the band singers backed off the boards since "A-Tisket A-Tasket" with Chick Webb's Orchestra. And she never stops. Ella is in a class by herself, in her particular groove.

Another great one was and is Peggy Lee. From the days she worked with Benny Goodman to the present she has been a tremendous standout. Plus she writes songs.

And then there's Judy Garland. When she was "straight" none could touch her. And her daughter, Liza Minnelli, is a tremendous legacy to show business. She is one of the greatest performers of any era.

However, all the female singers of the past put together, whether they worked with bands or never went near one, could not match the talent of Barbara Streisand. I go back a long way. I have reviewed all of the past era of big-name female singers as far back as Ruth Etting.

None match Streisand.

And she's also a female Sinatra in that she acts well and is into producing.

With that voice she doesn't need brains.

Compared to all the above, who really made history in the music business, the great majority of today's "singers" are what one would call caterwaulers.

That doesn't extend to all rock talent. There are solid performers and writers out there right now, but the good are so few that they stand out like sore thumbs. The trouble is, it appears, that when the good ones pile up a good poke as a result of the mountainous payoffs available, they tend to take it too easy, which emphasizes the impression that so much of the remainder is good only for the garbage heap.

There is only one modern groove that I enjoy. That's the instrumental, the releases that make the automotive boom-boxes vibrate as the neighborhood kids turn up the volume.

And I've heard some really great jazz and light jazz things on radio in recent years. Unfortunately, it is not appreciated enough to have more than one radio outlet per city spreading the message.

For a while in the early 70's I thought that Disco would again make musical life pleasant, but in short order it was absorbed into rock.

Generally though, today's music business performances and overall talent mark one of the few major industries in this whole wide world whose product has clearly and unquestionably deteriorated instead of improving.

And that's real sad in view of what might have been accomplished due to the great strides taken by the electronics industry in developing the equipment that reproduces sound.

But, as I complained elsewhere in this tome, the equipment makers do help the many, many modern "talents" who can't be good. They can be loud.

CHAPTER 46

Dancing

Dancing in the modern manner is somewhat different than it was during the Big Band Era. Routines like the Lindy Hop and the Peabody are lost arts in the 90's, except perhaps at dances set up for seniors, although that's doubtful in the upper ages.

Dances as they were known in the past are virtually nonexistent today, except perhaps for special affairs. In the west kids get along with what they call "House Dances," where a flock of youngsters get together, roll up the carpet and have fun. The dances they do mostly are called the "Hippety Hop" and "Freaking."

Most dancing all over the country, however, is a simple matter of getting out on the floor and each couple doing their own thing. In short, they simply move to the beat in any manner that comes to mind.

Loose-fitting clothes are the mode of dress. Formal or semi-formal outfits are long gone excepting for special events or affairs at hotel ballrooms.

Pity.

Enoch Light

As a bandleader, Enoch Light never rose above the secondary level. His orchestra's style kept him anchored in long-run hotel jobs such as the Taft Hotel, New York, with network broadcast wires, which gathered enough of a following to permit occasional one-night road tours.

On one run of road dates he had a head-on car collision that put him in a hospital bed for weeks. It's crazy to say that the crash was a godsend, but that's exactly what it turned out to be.

While recovering, Enoch re-evaluated his aims in life. The type of band he'd been leading was taking him nowhere. He had to devise a new approach. He began planning a record company, putting arrangements on paper and otherwise preparing for the day he could resume gainful work but avoid bandleading—at least in public.

Enoch formed the Grand Award record label, featuring no one but himself and the singer who worked with his road band. Using all standard songs he turned out a line of records that became highly successful, so successful that it attracted the attention of the American Broadcasting Company.

ABC had launched a recording division only a short time before Light debuted his Grand Award and its position was still not too strong. Consequently, ABC made Enoch an offer of $1,000,000 for his company, plus a contract to operate it as a separate entity.

The joker in the woodpile was that Light, in the meantime, had planned a second label called Command Records. He had cut his first sides, which looked tremendously promising, but had not yet released anything to the market. The Command approach was high-quality stereo sound, which was by then a known quantity to both record manufacturers and equipment manufacturers, but the major recording companies were still turning out the same old monaural recordings.

Enoch felt he had a valuable property in what he was developing on Command and desperately wanted to refuse the ABC bid. But the early work on Command was underwritten with Grand Award funds and there was no way he could legally keep Command for himself if he sold Grand Award to ABC.

But that million dollars in hand looked too good. He finally went through with the deal, throwing what already had been done to develop Command into the pot with Grand Award.

Light's initial release on Command was a tremendous stereo recording titled "Persuasive Percussion." It was a smash. A couple of years or so after its release it had reached five million dollars in sales and had been followed by a string of albums almost equally successful.

Not a bad deal for American Broadcasting.

CHAPTER 48

Finale

Ninety percent of rock music is a crime against the word "music" and 90 percent of the "performers" who feature it commit crimes against the word "talent."

Performers and purveyors of this blight on music and song call it entertainment. What sort of entertainment can it be when a member of Blind Melon, a group with a hit record, injects into its performance the "art" of stripping to the skin onstage and urinating, as happened during a recent concert in Vancouver, British Columbia?

And how about that great "performing artist" Madonna?

Or the world-renowned Michael Jackson, part of whose onstage entertainment is repeatedly stroking his crotch as he works. (His sister, La Toya, does the same thing.)

At this point the modern music world might invent a new word to describe what it puts before the public in the guise of "entertainment." It certainly isn't that. Whatever it is, it is at least partially responsible for the habits and violence of the younger generation.

Author, Robert Weaver, once wrote that nostagia isn't when you want to go back. Rather it's when you want to go back and know you can't....

Time, oh time, turn backward in your flight!